ACCIDENTS

IN NORTH AMERICAN MOUNTAINEERING

VOLUME 10 · NUMBER 4 · ISSUE 67
2014

AMERICAN ALPINE CLUB
GOLDEN, COLORADO

ALPINE CLUB OF CANADA
CANMORE, ALBERTA

 PAT GOODMAN

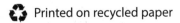
ISSN: 0065-028X
ISBN: 978-1-933056-85-2
ISBN (e-book): 978-1-933056-86-9

Manufactured in the United States. Published by: *The American Alpine Club, 710 Tenth Street, Suite 100, Golden, CO, 80401, www.americanalpineclub.org*

COVER IMAGES:

[**Front**] Grace Marx descending the upper reaches of McAllister Glacier after climbing Dorado Needle, North Cascades National Park, Washington. *Obadiah Reid*

[**Back**] YOSAR members lower down El Capitan to rescue the stranded Marc Venery and recover the body of his partner, Mason Robison, who fell to his death after a loose block cut his lead rope (see p.38). *Cheyne Lempe*

DEDICATION

THE 2014 EDITION OF *Accidents in North American Mountaineering* is dedicated to Jed Williamson, who edited this publication for 40 years, beginning in 1974. During that time he devoted countless hours, entirely without pay, toward collecting, editing, and sharing climbers' stories and lessons, in hopes of preventing needless tragedies. This is his final edition. Words cannot express our appreciation for Jed's extraordinary efforts on behalf of the climbing community.

ACCIDENTS IN NORTH AMERICAN MOUNTAINEERING

AMERICAN ALPINE CLUB

SAFETY ADVISORY COUNCIL, 2014
Aram Attarian, John Dill (NPS Ranger, Yosemite National Park), Chris Harder (NPS Ranger, Grand Teton National Park), and John E. (Jed) Williamson (Chair)

MANAGING EDITOR
John E. (Jed) Williamson

ASSOCIATE EDITOR
Aram Attarian

ASSISTANT EDITOR & ART DIRECTOR
Erik Rieger

COPY EDITORS
Joe Forrester, Erik Hansen, Jim Pasterczyk

KNOW THE ROPES CONTRIBUTORS
Dunham Gooding and Jason D. Martin
American Alpine Institute

PUBLICATIONS INTERN
Michiko Arai

ADDITIONAL THANKS
Leo Paik, Robert Speik, Mark Vermeal

AAC EXECUTIVE EDITOR
Dougald MacDonald

ALPINE CLUB OF CANADA

CHAIR, SAFETY COMMITTEE
Ernst M. Bergmann
safety@alpineclubofcanada.ca

CANADIAN CONTENT EDITOR
Robert Chisnall
anam@alpineclubofcanada.ca

JOHN SCURLOCK

CONTENTS

EDITORIAL

The 67th Annual Edition of
Accidents in North American Mountaineering

CANADA:

We thank the Alpine Club of Canada for submitting reports again this year. Robert Chisnall, an ACC member from Kinsgston, Ontario, was responsible for preparing the narratives.

UNITED STATES:

This will be the last issue for which I will be the managing editor. I took on this task 40 years ago at the request of William L. Putnam and Dr. Benjamin G. Ferris Jr. They were the leaders of the first two expeditions I went on, and were my sponsors for membership in the American Alpine Club in the early 1960s.

As a member of the AAC Safety Committee, which began in 1947, Dr. Ferris designed the current format of *Accidents in North American Mountaineering* and served as editor from 1952 to 1973. For the first 20 years, the report was between 20 and 30 pages long, reflecting how few climbers were active on this continent. In the early years, *Accidents* seemed to be lying in wait for the young, brash, incompetent, unsupervised, unregulated, and ill-equipped. When an experienced climber got into trouble, the analysis often began with such comments as, "It is hard to imagine how a man with so many years of experience (who fell to his death from a rappel) could have been so lax as to use such an inferior means of security, tied only with a single knot." Some things have barely changed.

When I began, reports were sent in by parks and occasionally by individuals. It was a cut-and-paste operation. About 500 copies were sent to the AAC membership and climbing clubs. The advent of computers, followed by the Internet, changed the entire process—for the better. Despite the dramatic increase in the size of the climbing community, we are able to ferret out the majority of incidents that result in serious injury and fatality. And the good news is that the annual number of these accidents, meanwhile, has held steady.

The AAC now prints nearly 20,000 copies of *Accidents*, and every report from all 66 previous editions is available online at *publications.americanalpineclub.org*. This book now has more images and illustrations and an annual instructional section. There are two changes that do not bode well, however. One is that many parks are redacting the names of climbers involved in accidents—primarily for HIPAA compliance—even though most of these names appear in newspapers and online, at websites such as Mountain Project and SuperTopo. Second is that rangers in some parks are no longer allowed to provide analyses of incidents. In the past, their insights have proven invaluable. Hopefully this will be only a temporary situation.

I am often asked whether all the data we have collected has been codified in such a manner that a statistical analysis could be done. The answer is that, given all the variables, only trends and patterns can be drawn from the tables. In Table III, for example, the leading cause of accidents appears to be falls on rock. Those falls are certainly what led to the injury or death, but the cause of the fall itself might be inadequate protection or falling rock. For anyone interested in taking a retrospective look at all the reports and recoding them, my file boxes are ready to be shipped COD!

Editing this publication has been a rewarding and educational journey. It has resulted in many unexpected diversions from my full-time work in education, including participation on boards of organizations such as NOLS, keynote speeches at conferences, safety reviews of programs, and full investigations of accidents resulting from climbing and other adventure activities.

I am grateful to everyone who has helped along the way. This includes many individuals no longer with us, all the current NPS rangers, and all individuals who send in or post their personal stories. There are too many people who are contributing to the current effort to list here. But I owe thanks to some special people who did more than their share during my watch: Aram Attarian, John Dill, Bob Irvine, Daryl Miller, Jim Detterline, Mike Gauthier, George Montopoli, Chris Harder, Jeff Scheetz, Robert Speik, Leo Paik, George and Mary Jane Sainsbury, Micki Canfield, Molly Allen, and Erik Hansen. My apologies to any I may have inadvertently omitted.

JOHN E. (JED) WILLIAMSON, *Managing Editor*

SUBMISSIONS

How to contribute incident reports to
Accidents in North American Mountaineering

Accidents in North American Mountaineering depends upon submissions from injured climbers, their partners, search and rescue organizations, and park officials. First-person reports or analysis of climbing accidents in the U.S. or Canada are always welcome. Visit **americanalpineclub.org/anam** or email **anam@americanalpineclub.org** to learn more.

RESCUE COVERAGE

THE AMERICAN ALPINE CLUB'S RESCUE BENEFITS

Since 1948, the American Alpine Club has published *Accidents in North American Mountaineering* annually, helping you prevent accidents on your own. But prevention isn't the only answer for coming out of a crisis alive.

Even when using great judgment, no one is immune to accidents. Whether you're close to home or climbing on a faraway expedition, AAC rescue coverage provides peace of mind in case something goes wrong.

Members of the American Alpine Club are automatically enrolled for $10,000 of rescue benefits that pay for out-of-pocket costs in the United States as well as Global Rescue services internationally. These services get used regularly. In 2013 alone, 19 AAC members were rescued across the globe.

COVERAGE DETAILS

Global Rescue ($5,000) — This benefit covers you anywhere in the world for rescue and evacuation by or under the direction of Global Rescue personnel. If you're injured beyond the trailhead, no matter the elevation, we will come to your aid. Members who want more than $5,000 of coverage can upgrade at a 5% discount by visiting americanalpineclub.org/rescue. **HOW TO USE THIS BENEFIT**: Call +1 (617) 459-4200 as soon as possible during an emergency.

Domestic Rescue ($5,000) — This benefit reimburses AAC members for out-of-pocket rescue costs in the United States. This benefit can be used in addition to the Global Rescue service. **HOW TO USE THIS BENEFIT**: File a claim within 30 days of evacuation by calling (303) 384-0110 or emailing claims@americanalpineclub.org. We will send you a check.

Activities covered include climbing, hiking, backcountry skiing, mountain biking and more—if it's human-powered on land and you're rescued, you're covered.

JOIN THE AMERICAN ALPINE CLUB
americanalpineclub.org/join
(303) 384-0110

Only active members may use these services. Immediately gain access to your $10,000 of rescue coverage by joining the American Alpine Club. As a member you also will be supporting the publication of this book, and you'll receive free copies of the latest *Accidents in North American Mountaineering* and *American Alpine Journal*, among many other benefits.

Don't leave yourself hanging.
$10,000 COVERAGE WITH MEMBERSHIP.

americanalpineclub.org/rescue

AAC member Menno Boermans

KNOW THE ROPES: SNOW CLIMBING

FUNDAMENTALS TO SAVE YOUR LIFE

By Dunham Gooding & Jason D. Martin, *American Alpine Institute*
Photos by Erik Rieger

"Slip on Snow." The phrase seems innocuous enough. It certainly doesn't sound like something that might lead to an injury or a fatality. But the reality of those three words in *Accidents* is quite different. If a slip or fall on snow appears in the heading of an abstract, it usually means that something terrible has happened. It might mean that someone has died.

In the last 10 years more than 300 snow travel accidents have been recorded in *Accidents in North American Mountaineering*. Many, but not all, of these accidents

CAUSES OF SNOW TRAVEL ACCIDENTS
2004–2013

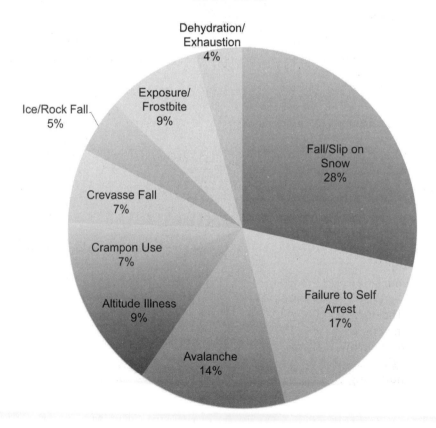

Dehydration/
Exhaustion
4%

Exposure/
Frostbite
9%

Ice/Rock Fall
5%

Fall/Slip on
Snow
28%

Crevasse Fall
7%

Crampon Use
7%

Failure to Self
Arrest
17%

Altitude Illness
9%

Avalanche
14%

were precipitated by deficient equipment or skills, including "Improper Crampon Use" or "Failure to Self Arrest"; others by illness, exhaustion, or injury; and yet others were the result of objective hazards like avalanches, rockfall, or icefall. Many, but not all, of these accidents could have been avoided had the climbers developed a better understanding of the skills required to move over snow—a dynamic and dangerous setting.

Effective snow travel is a baseline skill that is often overlooked by beginners and advanced climbers alike. In many cases, climbing clubs and even some professional guide services do not spend adequate time teaching effective movement and fall avoidance on snow. This leaves all of these climbers—beginner to advanced—open to the possibility of making mistakes that result in injury to themselves or others.

In the following pages, we will discuss the baseline skills that every mountain traveler must master in order to move efficiently over snow, maximize safety, and minimize risk. For both ascending and descending snow slopes, there are two main techniques that we will address: using your feet and using your ice axe. Effective snow travel requires synchronization of both techniques, matching those techniques to the proper terrain, and ensuring the equipment matches as well. Finally, we'll briefly discuss strategies for choosing the route, time of ascent, and when to belay or unrope on snow.

USING YOUR FEET

Good footwork is the first line of security against slips on snow. And good footwork requires mountaineering boots, with rigid or semi-rigid soles and ample lugs for traction. (Inadequate footwear is frequently a contributing factor in snow-travel incidents reported in *Accidents*.) In soft snow, without crampons, there are three recommended techniques. All three can be adapted for use with crampons when snow conditions require it.

Duck Walk

Lower-angle, soft to mildly hard spring and summer snow often allows one to travel effectively without crampons. In this terrain—often up to 35 degrees—the most effective technique is the "duck walk."

Splay your toes out so that

[This page] The duck walk is best used on slopes up to about 35°. Cutting into the slope with the boot's edge gives security to the step when not using crampons.

your feet make a V in the snow. As you move up the slope, feet splayed, kick the surface of the snow, using the inside edge of your boot to cut a platform. Move your weight onto the platform as soon as you have cut it, and then repeat the process with your other foot. If your little platform gives way under your weight, kick again and create subsequent steps with a more vigorous swing of your foot to cut deeper into the slope.

Step Kicking

As the angle increases, you will find it more comfortable to kick steps straight into the slope. Step kicking straight up the fall line is more strenuous than moving on a diagonal, but it is an effective way to increase your security. If the snow is consolidated but soft enough to kick good steps, you will have a good platform on which to stand. You will also be facing the slope, which is an excellent position from which to perform a quick self-arrest in the event of a slip.

Diagonal Ascent

If the snow is not soft enough to kick good steps, but is too steep for the duck walk, you may wish to make a diagonal ascent, switchbacking up the slope. The standard technique for moving up a steep slope at a diagonal is to employ a crossover step.

When moving up at a diagonal, there will always be a downhill foot (on the side of your body away from the slope) and an uphill foot (on the side closest to the slope). To move up the slope, cross your downhill foot above your uphill foot and then step up. Now bring the other foot around from behind to return to the uphill position. Once you've completed this crossover step, you should be in the same position from which you started. You'll note that when you're in the

[This page, top] Step kicking is relatively straightforward in softer snow conditions, yielding a solid platform for footing. [This page, bottom] When the snow gets too hard and/or steep for duck walking or step kicking, it's best to move diagonally up the slope, cutting the boot's edge into the snow.

awkward crossed position you're "out of balance." When you're in your original position, you're "in balance." If you're using an ice axe to increase stability, it should be on the uphill side of your body and you should only move it when you're in balance. Only stop to rest when in balance.

If you have trouble keeping track of which position is in balance and which is not, remember that the position that tends to make you face the slope is out of balance, and the one that tends to face you out slightly from the slope is in balance.

In order to change the direction of your ascent, bring your downhill foot up into an out-of-balance step, and then match that foot in a V position with your other foot, creating a duck stance. From there, make an in-balance step and kick a stance with the new uphill foot, pointing in the new direction. Note that the duck stance is always in balance, so it is possible to switch the ice axe from one hand to the other at any time while securely in that stance.

In harder snow you will have to shear each stance by cutting into the slope with a brisk forward swing of your foot, using a combination of the edge and the sole of your boot. In good conditions you should be able to cut your foot into the slope using a single movement. On hard snow you may need to kick several times to cut an appropriate stance.

Effective Crampon Use

In the past, a number of climbing clubs taught that crampon use was "required" for glacier travel. Thankfully this practice is far less common today, but there are still a lot of climbers out there who believe this to be true.

The reality is you should only wear crampons when the conditions require it. Crampons are dangerous. You can stab yourself with them or catch a point on a piece of clothing and trip. Crampons are required only when you walk or climb on firm snow or ice. It doesn't matter whether you are on a glacier or not. If wearing crampons doesn't increase your security, you should stow them until the conditions change.

It is common to start a climb early in the morning when snow slopes are thoroughly frozen. In a temperate climate, as the day unfolds, rising temperatures and direct sunlight on the snow can rapidly change frozen snow to soft snow or mush. Recognize when crampons are no longer needed and take them off.

When wet snow begins to ball up on the bottom of a crampon, the possibility of slipping and falling becomes very real. If the snow is soft enough, consider removing your crampons. In some cases a thin layer of wet snow on top of ice or hard snow makes crampons essential. For this reason mountaineers should always employ crampons equipped with anti-bot plates. These plastic inserts help keep snow from balling up between the crampon spikes.

The crampons you choose should be compatible with your boot and should be appropriate for the objective. If you elect to wear crampons with a toe bail or a heel bail/clipper, confirm that the rand/welts on the boot are appropriate for these crampons before you leave for the mountains. Try pulling down on the center bar and pulling the front points side to side. Does the crampon shift or lose contact with the boot, even if the sole is flexed? If the crampons do not fit securely, they must be adjusted or a different crampon/boot combination should be chosen. Never ignore a badly fitting crampon or just hope that it will improve.

Tripping is a significant hazard with crampons, often a result of the frontpoints snagging on clothing or gear. It's not uncommon to see climbers wearing gaiters on the wrong feet, with the buckles on the inside of the legs—this provides a prominent place for a frontpoint to catch, causing a stumble. Be sure extra crampon straps are tucked away and that—if not wearing gaiters—the cuff of your pants has a low profile. (Many modern mountaineering pants have grommets to attach elastic cords that run under the boots, eliminating the need for bulky gaiters.)

Once you put on your crampons, you should continually focus on good technique, using thoughtful and controlled steps. Running down a slope, climbing while tired, or stepping out of balance are all good ways to either trip or stab yourself with a crampon point.

[This page] On lower-angled slopes, French technique minimizes fatigue. The ankles must flex to engage all the bottom points of the crampons.

French Technique (Flat Foot)

French technique is the art of flexing the ankle so provide purchase for all of the crampon points on the bottom of your boot. Most modern crampons have 10 points on the bottom and two frontpoints on each toe. An individual employing proper French technique will engage all 10 of the bottom points to create a high level of security in the step. This is also referred to as the flat-foot technique or, in French, *pieds à plat*.

In hard snow or icy conditions the flat-foot technique may be used in combination with both the duck walk and a diagonal ascent. The techniques are the same as described without crampons, with one significant difference: You must flex your ankles sideways so that all of the crampon points bite into the surface.

American Technique (Hybrid or Pied Troisième)

As the slope angle increases (usually above 45°) it becomes difficult to maintain diagonal French technique without shifting the toe of your boots so radically downhill—in order to engage all of the crampons' bottom teeth—that you end up walking up the slope backward. Moving this way is physically demanding and isn't terribly secure.

Instead, shift one foot out of the French stance and engage the frontpoints in the snow. The other foot should remain flat-footed against the slope. This technique allows you to face the slope and move quickly, while saving the strength in your calves. As the calf in the frontpoint position tires, simply switch feet and allow the pumped calf to rest in a flat-footed French position while the rested foot and leg take over the frontpointing.

Austrian Technique (Frontpointing)

The third crampon method is the Austrian technique, or frontpointing. This technique is reserved for very steep angles—usually in excess of 70°—though some climbers prefer it on somewhat lower-angled terrain.

Frontpointing requires one to kick their crampons straight into the slope, and then to drop the heels approximately 10° below a level stance. Dropping the heels engages not only the frontpoints but the next two points on the crampon as

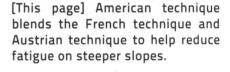

[This page] American technique blends the French technique and Austrian technique to help reduce fatigue on steeper slopes.

well. The result is that a climber stands on four points, instead of just two, which increases the stability of the placements.

Frontpoint crampon technique tires the calf muscles, and because fatigue is a significant contributor to slips and falls on snow and ice, climbers should use the American technique rather than frontpointing whenever it's reasonable.

USING AN ICE AXE

Many mountaineers tend to see the ice axe primarily as a tool for self-arrest. But an ice axe should be used primarily to increase security while climbing, in order to decrease the likelihood of a fall. Being able to execute a good self-arrest is important, but the first goal is always not to fall.

Ice Axe Choice

For mountaineering routes, a straight-shafted axe with a gently curved pick and no molded plastic grips or handles, roughly 60 to 70cm long (depending on the climber's height), will provide the most versatility and security for snow travel, self-arrest techniques, and creating snow anchors.

However, many climbers opt for shorter technical tools for alpine routes and ice climbs, even those that may require serious snow travel en route or during the approach or descent. Some technical tools work better than others in such applications. Consider tools with lower-profile finger guards and grips, a generous spike, and a less radical curve to the shaft.

Leashes

In most mountaineering settings, there is no compelling reason to leash an ice axe to your wrist. The tool is always to be carried in the uphill hand, and using a leash requires the climber to switch the leash to the other hand every time he changes direction on a diagonal ascent. This takes time, decreases security, and takes focus off the task at hand. In most settings, the danger of dropping an ice axe is lower than the risk of destabilization during a transition.

However, using a leash makes sense in contexts where the likelihood of a drop increases. For example, when wearing mittens in extremely cold weather or on high-altitude climbs, a leash is imperative because of the lack of dexterity. (In some cases, it may be preferable to tether the axe directly to your harness, because switching a leash with bulky mittens and clothing can be nearly impossible.) When climbing steep ice, wearing some kind of leash or tether makes sense, because dropping an axe in such a setting could be catastrophic.

How To Hold the Axe: Cane Position vs. Self-Arrest Position

While climbing moderately steep snow, mountaineers have two primary choices of ice axe positions: carrying the axe in the cane position, with the pick forward, or carrying the axe in the self-arrest position, with the pick backward. It is not uncommon to hear climbers argue about which is better. But it's clear which way is better: The cane position is better when you are actively climbing the mountain, and the self-arrest position is better when you are actively falling off the mountain.

All joking aside, the cane position (*piolet canne*) provides more stability and should be used in most cases while ascending, for two major reasons. First, it's easier to firmly set the axe's spike in the snow when you have the palm of your hand seated comfortably on the flat surface of the adze. Placing the spike effectively in hard snow with the axe in the self-arrest position will eventually bruise the palm of your hand on the narrow edge of the pick, causing you to be less aggressive with the axe. Second, as the angle of the slope increases, it is more natural to transition from the cane position into one of the dagger positions with the axe.

Obviously, one will be slightly slower to move into a self-arrest with an ice axe in the cane position. Some would argue that this compromises one's safety. But the best way to address that compromise is to practice self-arrest from the cane position until it is second nature and can be employed as effectively as from the self-arrest position. Switch to the self-arrest position only when there is an obvious danger—like crossing a heavily crevassed area on a rope team or traversing a very steep slope—when the climber must be prepared to self-arrest.

[This page, left] The ice axe held in the cane position. [This page, right] The axe held in the self-arrest position. There are reasons to use both, and climbers should become comfortable with each.

Self-Belay Position (Piolet Manche)

The self-belay or "deep plunge" position is a secure technique for steep snow climbing. The axe is pushed down vertically into the snow as deeply as possible, while you continue to hold the head of the tool. The head of the axe becomes a handhold. (In French, *manche* means "handle" or "sleeve." Imagine the shaft of the axe down in a sleeve of snow that will keep it in place, creating a good handle.)

There are two ways to hold the axe while employing this technique. In softer snow, when the majority of the shaft is buried, you can hold the head of the axe with both hands. This is very secure.

If the snow is too hard or icy for the axe to penetrate very far, it isn't effective to have both hands on the head because in a slip you may simply lever the spike out. Instead, one hand can be placed on the head of the axe while the other grips the shaft at the point where it disappears into the snow. In the event of a slip, the hand on top of the axe should push forward, while counter pressure is applied to the hand that is lower on the shaft. In other words, you should be pushing in on the top and pulling out with the hand just above the spike. If pressures are applied correctly, the slip will be arrested by this technique before it becomes a fall.

[This page, top] The self-belay position with both hands on the head of the ice axe works well in soft snow. On harder snow it's often better to position the second hand lower on the shaft.

Anchor Position (Piolet Ancre)

Occasionally a climber will need to make a quick placement with the pick of his axe in order to pull over a bulge or assist with a crevasse crossing. To do this, hold the axe in your dominant hand just above the spike and swing it over your head like you're pounding in a nail. Right at the end of the swing, flick your wrist forward; this will allow the pick to bite more deeply. Once the pick is placed, you can use both the shaft and the head of the axe as handholds while you climb up over your obstacle.

Low, Middle and High Dagger Positions

On steep snow and ice, most commonly on terrain between 45° and 70°, one or more of the dagger positions may be useful. The climber holds the ice axe at the top of the shaft or on the head while seating the pick of the axe in the snow. Dagger positions work well in hard snow or on névé, but are less effective on hard ice, where the only way to create an effective pick placement is to swing the axe.

The first of these three techniques is the low dagger position, or *piolet panne*. In this position, place the palm of your hand on the top of the adze as you press the pick into the slope at waist level. This is a quick technique that doesn't require any changes to the way you hold your ice axe, assuming you started out in the cane position, but it doesn't feel as secure as some other techniques because

[This page, bottom] In solid snow, an axe in anchor position offers a good handhold.

the pick is so low. It will be most useful for downclimbing.

In the middle dagger position (*piolet appui*), place your hand on the shaft of the axe right below the head. This position allows you to push the pick into the slope more forcefully, making each stick feel more secure.

In the high dagger position (*piolet poignard*), hold the head of the axe, wrapping your fingers over the pick in front of the shaft while you wrap your thumb under the adze behind the shaft. To place the axe, reach high and stab the pick into the slope. A high dagger placement often provides better security on very steep slopes than the other two dagger positions.

Self-Arrest

Failure to self-arrest is a common contributor to the incidents found in these pages, and many climbers are almost obsessively fixated on their ice axe as a tool to arrest a fall. But many times a slope is too steep or the snow too hard or icy for an effective self-arrest. Think of an icy slope of 40° or more and

[This page, top] The axe placed in low dagger position allows for a quick step on steeper snow.

you'll get the picture: The falling climber starts sliding too quickly to control a slide.

When a fall takes place, a mistake has already been made. Therefore, as we've said before, although it is important to practice self-arrest it is perhaps more important to practice the art of not falling. Work on proper foot technique, practice using the ice axe as an aid to decrease the likelihood of a fall, and develop situational awareness by paying attention to your surroundings and managing risk on exposed terrain.

Your risk management strategy should take into account both the condition of the snow and the angle of the slope. In soft snow conditions, even on 40° terrain, a self-arrest may be effective. But in icy conditions, even on a lower-angled slope, a self-arrest may well be unsuccessful. If it doesn't appear that a self-arrest will be feasible, you may have to alter your climbing strategy, including roping up and belaying or choosing an alternate line.

Depending on the circumstances, you may end up sliding down the slope after a slip in any number of different ways: feet-first on your back, head-first on your stomach, etc. It doesn't matter how you fall, the goal is the same: Roll into a self-arrest position with the shaft of the axe across your body, place the pick in the snow, look away from the adze, then torque the spike up while lifting with your legs. This should bury the pick deep in the slope's surface and bring you to a stop. It's beyond the scope of this article to explain self-arrest in depth: Seek

instruction and practice repeatedly. Find a low-consequence slope and take a variety of mock slips and falls in varying positions to get the hang of it. Building good instincts takes repetition.

Most climbers practice self-arrest with a standard alpine piolet. These ice axes were designed with self-arrest in mind and work well for it. Shorter, technical ice tools are not as easy to manipulate into the self-arrest position, and the picks may skitter off hard snow or ice. Those who climb with technical tools should practice self-arrest with such tools until it is second nature.

One great debate over the practice of self-arrest is whether the climber should kick his feet up during an arrest, in order to ensure he doesn't get flipped over by his crampons, or whether he should bury his toes into the snow no matter the cost. Many climbing clubs still teach the former technique, whereas most guides now teach the latter.

In the event of a fall, the most important thing is to stop. Style points don't matter. Indeed, even injury doesn't matter. What matters is that you fight with everything that you have in order to arrest a fall.

DESCENDING ON SNOW

Many snow-climbing accidents occur while descending. Often this is because the climber is tired and not paying attention to the surroundings and the conditions

[This page] Bury the pick deeply in a self-arrest, keeping the axe head near your shoulder. Push upward with your knees to get more weight onto the axe. Many guides now teach that you should dig your toes into the snow, choosing additional braking power over the risk of snagging a toe and flipping backward.

under foot. It is important to stay alert on the way down, and to focus both on the slope below you as well as on your feet.

Plunge Step

The plunge step is an aggressive and direct way to descend a slope of soft snow. Think of it as reversed step kicking. To do it effectively, bend your knees slightly, spread your feet shoulder width apart, and step straight downhill, striking the slope with the heel of your boot. The heel will cut into the snow and create a platform for the rest of the boot.

In harder snow conditions, it is imperative that the heel aggressively hits the slope on every step and that the toe is pointed slightly upward. Try to plunge down and kick back to achieve the proper step. Often people who are not aggressive plunge-steppers may slip and then become more timid in their steps, which leads to more falls and more timidity. If you fall once, don't back off—be more aggressive in your steps to ensure that your heel cuts deeply enough to create a secure step.

Most climbers will feel comfortable with the plunge step in soft conditions on slopes up to about 40°. In semi-hard conditions, aggressive plunge-stepping should be reserved for slopes that are 35° or under. If the conditions are too hard to plunge-step securely, descending with crampons is a better option.

[This page, top] Soft snow makes descending relatively easy, but when the slope steepens or the snow is harder, an aggressive plunge step or downclimbing is required.

[This page, bottom] Lift your toes a bit to cut a good step for your boot.

Shuffle Step

If the terrain is steeper or more exposed, climbers may resort to the shuffle step to increase the security of their descent. This technique is not fast, but is very secure and can be done with crampons on or off, depending on the conditions.

[This page, top] Shuffling downhill. Note that the climber's axe is on the uphill side, ready for self-arrest.

Face perpendicular to the slope and step down with your downhill foot. Now move your uphill foot down into the step your downhill foot occupied a moment earlier. Your ice axe should be in your uphill hand in the cane or self-arrest position, with the spike planted firmly in the snow. Once your feet are next to one another, move the ice axe down, planting the spike once more.

Downclimb

Downclimbing steep slopes on frontpoints or with American (*pied troisième*) technique is often faster than setting up a rappel. Indeed, in conditions where it's hard to build a good rappel anchor, downclimbing may even be safer.

Some climbers might feel comfortable downclimbing 60° snow, while others wouldn't dream of it. If one member of a team is uncomfortable downclimbing a given slope, it may be better to belay him and then solo down. Alternately, you might consider setting up a rappel for the entire team.

Descending with Crampons

The biggest thing to remember when descending with crampons is that it is easy to trip over a gaiter, shoelace, or pant leg while walking or plunge-stepping downhill. For this reason, it is important to splay the toes of your crampons out a little bit on the descent and keep your two feet away from each other. Also, beware of snow balling up under the crampons. From an in-balance position, knock snow off the crampons by banging the sides of them with your ice axe or by kicking one crampon against the side of the other.

[This page, bottom] How NOT to descend: The climber is out of balance with his weight too far forward.

Glissading

Many mountaineers ascending lower-angled mountains look forward to the adventure of glissading down snow slopes after their climb. There are three types of glissade that a climber can employ: standing glissade, three-point glissade, and sitting glissade. But losing control of a glissade is a contributing factor to many accidents. Following four guidelines can help minimize the risk.

Never glissade with crampons on. People get injured every year because they wear crampons while glissading. If you're wearing crampons, it's probably icy, and if it's icy you probably shouldn't be glissading. Second, and perhaps more importantly, if you're wearing crampons while glissading quickly, you could easily snag a spike on hard snow or ice, with the possibility of breaking an ankle or leg.

Never glissade while tied into a rope team. If you are roped up, it should be because there are hazards that require a measured and controlled approach. Sliding down the hill is the antithesis of measure and control.

Never glissade on a glacier. If you are on a "wet" glacier, then it is likely that you are roped up to manage the crevasse hazard. The preceding rule states that glissading while roped up is never advised. If you're not roped up, glissading on a glacier opens the possibility of a crevasse fall, which almost always has severe consequences.

Always make sure you can see where you're going. You should not glissade if there is any fog or rollovers to negotiate. Glissading off a cliff, into a moat, or onto talus is a terrible way to end your day.

[This page] A sitting glissade, the most common and stable of the various types. The climber here can be seen controlling the speed of his slide with the spike of his ice axe. His top hand grasps the head of the ice axe in self-arrest position.

SNOW CLIMBING STRATEGIES

There are many snow-climbing situations where climbers may choose to move together while roped to one another. The most common is to protect against a crevasse fall. But this technique also may be used to protect a team from a fall down snow or ice through the use of a running belay.

To rig a running belay, the leader places snow or ice protection and then clips the rope to it. As the second approaches, he can either clip the rope behind him as he passes the protection to safeguard the remaining climbers or—if on a two-person team—remove the protection. If an individual on the team falls, he may pull the others off, but the protection between the climbers will theoretically arrest the fall, limiting the damage of the incident.

In some settings, it might be more efficient and perhaps even safer for the climbers on a team to unrope and "solo" a slope. Imagine a slope that's not steep enough to require belaying individual pitches, and that, in order to move quickly, you make a team decision not to employ a running belay. On steep or icy slopes where self-arrest is unlikely, the slip of a single climber roped to the rest of the group could result in the loss of the entire team. In such a situation, it might be safer for the individual climbers to unrope.

The decision to unrope should not be made lightly. First, you must consider the reasons that you employed a rope in the first place and determine if those risk factors are still valid. Second, you must feel confident in the ability of each member of your team to solo the slope safely. If you have any doubts about a team member's skill, you should continue to use the rope and either employ running belays or stop and belay each climber up or down the slope.

Timing the Climb

Many accidents take place because of unstable snow. In a spring or summer context, this often includes the combination of wet slide avalanches, collapsing cornices, and weak snow bridges over crevasses. These dangers may be mitigated by an early morning ascent.

On glaciated peaks and on peaks with a lot of objective hazard, it's not uncommon for spring and summer climbing teams to leave camp between midnight and 4 a.m. Teams should estimate how long it will take to climb the mountain and descend, and then plan a departure early enough to ensure they are off the snow before the sun dangerously warms the slopes.

During the colder months and in colder regions, parties often elect to climb during the day. The cooler temperatures provide a margin of safety that is similar to that experienced by night climbers in the spring and summer. However, it is not uncommon for temperatures to warm and for parties to have to adapt their schedules to the weather. Those who do not adapt to the conditions put themselves at risk.

Ideally, mountaineers will encounter firm, easily climbed snow during the ascent and softer snow—but not *too* wet or soft—for a rapid, easy descent. Timing a climb to find such conditions is a key aspect of the craft of mountaineering.

Making Good Choices

Effectively moving on snow involves a matrix of skills and decisions. An individual who has mastered such techniques will not be immune from appearing in these pages under the heading that reads "fall on snow," but he or she will certainly be much less likely to have an accident.

Most importantly, a casual, "make it up as you move along" approach to snow travel is not safe. You will most successfully deal with each slope angle and each type of snow or ice under foot by applying a specific technique, and

Timing a climb is just as important as good technique. Although these climbers started early, they encountered new snow that softened rapidly as the day warmed. Wet-snow avalanche debris adorns the cirque in the background.

the techniques required can change repeatedly over a relatively short distance. When you have learned and practiced the complete repertoire of fundamental skills discussed here, you always will be making "best choices" for each step of your climbs.

ABOUT THE AUTHORS

Dunham Gooding founded the American Alpine Institute in 1975 and has taught courses and guided expeditions in the Cascades, Canada, Ecuador, Bolivia, and Patagonia. He has served as chairman of the National Summit Committee on Mountain Rescue, president of the American Mountain Guides Association (AMGA), and president of the Outdoor Industry Association. Jason D. Martin is the director of operations and a senior guide at the American Alpine Institute. He is on the board of directors of the AMGA and has written two guidebooks and co-authored *Rock Climbing: The AMGA Single Pitch Manual.*

Special thanks to Bryan Simon, who helped analyze snow-travel accidents reported in the past decade of *Accidents* editions.

DANGER ZONES: MT. RAINIER

WHERE & WHY ACCIDENTS HAPPEN

By Michiko Arai

THE MAJESTIC, 14,410-FOOT VOLCANO of Mt. Rainier, just 55 miles from Seattle, is one of the most popular mountaineering destinations in North America. Lined by massive glaciers on all sides, the mountain is attempted by about 10,000 people a year. It's also the site of numerous accidents and close calls. More than 95 mountaineers have died on Rainier's slopes, including the tragic loss of six climbers in late May 2014 after an avalanche high on Liberty Ridge.

This article aims to prevent future tragedies by analyzing the accident history of popular routes. We reviewed more than 110 reports from Mt. Rainier in *Accidents in North American Mountaineering* over the past 20 years. In addition, we examined the causes of climbing fatalities from 1984 through 2013, as tracked by Mountrainierclimbing.us. The data reveal accident trends on specific routes, suggesting how climbers might best prepare to avoid future incidents.

Geologically, Mt. Rainier sits on the Ring of Fire around the Pacific Ocean basin. Geologists consider Mt. Rainier to be an active, potentially dangerous volcano. More immediately, heavy snowfall and highly active glaciers shape the challenging terrain of the mountain.

Although there are more than 40 routes and variations up Mt. Rainier, the vast majority of climbers follow two lines: 1) up the Muir Snowfield to Camp Muir, followed by a summit attempt via the Ingraham Glacier or Disappointment Cleaver, or 2) the Emmons/Winthrop Glaciers route above Camp Schurman. With one prominent exception—Liberty Ridge—most accidents occur along these routes. As former climbing ranger Mike Gauthier notes in *Mt. Rainier: A Climbing Guide*, climbers tend to underestimate the difficulty of moderate routes.

As on any climb, hazards on Rainier fall into two categories: objective and subjective. Subjective hazards include errors on the climber's part, such as inadequate experience, lack of fitness, and poor technique. Objective hazards include rockfall, icefall, storms, and avalanches. Although climbers can minimize subjective hazards through training and practice, many accidents result from a combination of factors. For example, an unfit climber may not be able to make it up and down the mountain before a warm afternoon increases the risk of rockfall or icefall. Accidents often have multiple layers of causes: The failure to keep snow from balling up on crampons causes a slip, which ends in a crevasse fall, which leads to injury or hypothermia.

Although storms and poor visibility are not often the immediate cause of

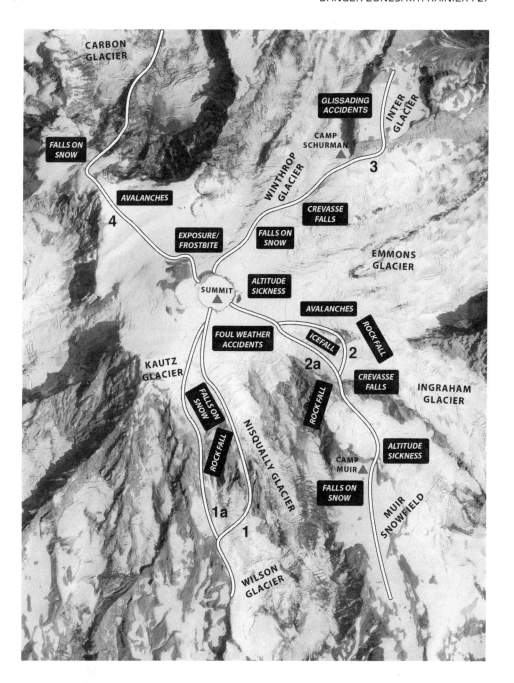

Mt. Rainier from ca 40,000 feet. The black boxes mark areas where acccidents of various types occur more frequently. (Note that accidents of each type have been recorded elsewhere on the mountain, too.) Notable accident-prone routes: 1) Fuhrer Finger. 1a) Kautz Glacier. 2) Disappointment Cleaver. 2a) Ingraham Glacier Direct. 3) Emmons/Winthrop Glaciers. 4) Liberty Ridge. *Google Earth*

MOST POPULAR ROUTES
Total number of climbers, 2006–2013

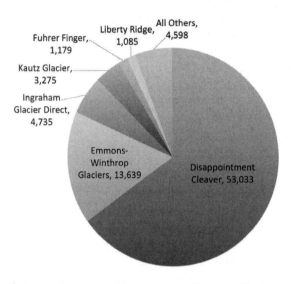

Fuhrer Finger, 1,179
Liberty Ridge, 1,085
All Others, 4,598
Kautz Glacier, 3,275
Ingraham Glacier Direct, 4,735
Emmons-Winthrop Glaciers, 13,639
Disappointment Cleaver, 53,033

an injury or fatality on Rainier, climbers should be aware that unexpected bad weather may occur anywhere on the mountain. Clouds, fog, and snow frequently contribute to the gravity of accidents and delay search and rescue efforts. July and August often bring stable weather, and these months see the most summit success. However, rain can fall high on the mountain in summer, causing treacherous footing when the freezing level drops.

Falls on snow and ice cause the most accidents on Rainier, especially on the Emmons/Winthrop Glaciers, Liberty Ridge, Ingraham Glacier, Disappointment Cleaver, and Kautz Glacier routes, and on Muir Snowfield. Climbers can avoid falling by learning the proper techniques for roped glacier travel, self-arrest, and climbing in crampons, trying more modest glacial routes to gain experience, and choosing appropriate partners. (See "Know the Ropes" in this edition.) Crevasse falls are most common on the Ingraham Glacier, Emmons Glacier, and near Camp Muir. Glissading accidents occur most often on Emmons Glacier, near Camp Muir, on the Muir Snowfield, and on the Inter Glacier.

Over the past 20 years of *Accidents*, Liberty Ridge, Ingraham Glacier, Disappointment Cleaver, and the Kautz Glacier have shown the greatest risk of avalanche, rockfall, and icefall. Mountaineers should attempt to climb these routes on colder days to decrease the risk of falling rocks and ice. Moving quickly and efficiently decreases exposure and risk of getting stuck.

Finally, climbers can decrease the risk of altitude illnesses and hypothermia by training appropriately, starting the climb healthy and hydrated, and properly acclimatizing.

Muir Snowfield and Camp Muir

Though it is not as steep as the upper mountain, the Muir Snowfield is the scene of many accidents, often involving climbers, hikers, or skiers unprepared for the conditions they'll encounter, including icy snow and whiteouts. It's not uncommon for people to wander to one side of the normal route and get into trouble. Crevasse falls occur, especially to the side of the main route and near Camp Muir (10,080'). Despite the relatively low elevation in this area, altitude sickness, hypothermia, and frostbite affect a number of climbers. Bottom line: Even the seemingly casual approach to Camp Muir must be viewed as a true mountaineering challenge, requiring appropriate preparation and equipment, including the ability to navigate in very limited visibility.

Disappointment Cleaver / Ingraham Glacier Direct

Two-thirds of aspiring Rainier climbers attempt the Disappointment Cleaver or neighboring Ingraham Glacier Direct route. Many accidents and illnesses occur here, including falls on snow or ice, crevasse falls, and avalanches. The deadliest accident in Rainier's history occurred just below Disappointment Cleaver in 1981, when an avalanche, likely caused by serac fall, wiped out 11 climbers. Falling ice on the Ingraham Glacier has been the cause of several other incidents. On or below Disappointment Cleaver, rockfall has caused several accidents. There is also a disproportionately high incidence of altitude illnesses.

Emmons/Winthrop Glaciers

This route, the second most popular on Rainier, is attempted only a quarter as often as Disappointment Cleaver. Yet it has seen about the same number of accidents and fatalities in the past 30 years. Although it is the least technical route up Rainier, the Emmons/Winthrop climbs 10,000 feet and is physically arduous. Climbers must arrive with adequate fitness and stay hydrated in order to avoid sickness and exhaustion. More than one-third of the falls reported on Rainier in the past two decades have occurred here, especially as tired climbers descend from the upper mountain. Since the route travels across glaciers with enormous crevasses, falling climbers frequently fall into slots. The Emmons/Winthrop has been relatively free of avalanche or falling ice, suggesting that if climbers can stay on their feet they will likely have a successful climb.

CLIMBING FATALITIES BY ROUTE

Total Fatalities, 1984-2013

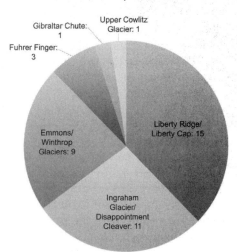

CLIMBING FATALITIES BY ACCIDENT CAUSE

Percentage of Fatalities, 1984-2013

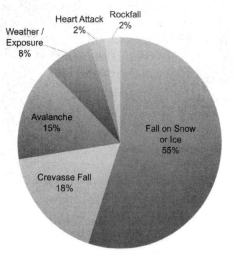

Liberty Ridge

This remote and difficult route is statistically the most dangerous on Rainier. Falls on snow or ice and avalanches have caused the most accidents. In addition, many accidents reported near the summit (Liberty Cap) or on the Emmons Glacier are actually the result of Liberty Ridge climbers becoming exhausted, hypothermic, or stranded by severe weather. (Most climbers traverse over 14,112-foot Liberty Cap and descend the Emmons/Winthrop Glaciers route.) This route's commitment level requires an excellent forecast and low avalanche hazard, the ability to climb moderately steep ice with heavy loads, having the right navigational tools and skills, and carrying the equipment and food/fuel reserves necessary to sit out a storm near the top.

Summit Area

Whichever route climbers attempt, the crater rim and the slopes below are statistically dangerous. Severe weather and poor visibility strand climbers, leading to hypothermia, frostbite, and other injuries. There have been several instances of mountaineers mistakenly believing they could find warm shelter in the steam vents near the crater. It's crucial to carry adequate bivouac gear and food to the top—don't be tempted to leave your survival gear at high camp. Unsurprisingly, altitude-related illness is fairly common near the summit. Falls also are not uncommon on the relatively low-angle ground around the crater rim. Exhaustion, severe weather, or lack of visibility each present sufficient reason to turn back before getting into trouble near the summit.

Kautz Glacier / Fuhrer Finger

The relatively isolated routes on the south side, above the Wilson and Nisqually glaciers, attract about 5 percent of Rainier climbers, looking for moderately difficult and less crowded alternatives to the most popular climbs. In addition to the usual hazards—falls, crevasses, avalanche—icefall and rockfall are notable in the accident record, particularly on the Kautz Glacier. A helmet is mandatory, even low on the route, and choosing a protected bivouac site mid-route is paramount.

THERE IS NO SUBSTITUTE for training and real-world practice before attempting big, glaciated mountains. Nonetheless, excellent information can be found in the books *Climbing Mt. Rainier*, by Fred Beckey and Alex Van Steen; *Mount Rainier: A Climbing Guide*, by Mike Gauthier; and *The Challenge of Rainier*, by Dee Molenaar. In addition, the National Park Service mountaineering webpage for Rainier (Nps.gov/mora/planyourvisit/climbing-2.htm) offers helpful trip-planning advice. Mountrainierclimbing.blogspot.com, a ranger-run website, is a great source of recent route information.

ACCIDENTS & ANALYSES

LEARN FROM OTHERS' MISTAKES

Cheyne Lempe

UNITED STATES

ALASKA

FALL INTO CREVASSE – TRAVELING UNROPED ON A GLACIER
St. Elias Range, Middle Peak

At the end of March, I (Colin Haley, 28) left for a climbing trip in Alaska's St. Elias Range with Portlanders John Frieh and Daniel Harro. We were flown into the range by Paul Claus midday on April 1. We spent a few hours setting up our base camp and then went for a short ski up-glacier to scope our objective. About 20 minutes out of camp, I suddenly broke through a totally hidden crevasse and fell approximately 15 meters, ricocheting off the walls of the crevasse.

We had left for our leisurely ski with essentially no equipment, so Daniel immediately skied back to camp to fetch a rope, crampons, ice tools, and harnesses. I was able to climb out of the crevasse with a top-rope (and even managed to rescue my skis and poles). Fortunately, I escaped any truly serious injuries. Unfortunately, however, I had a fractured cheekbone and my trip was over. We skied back to camp and the next morning I flew off the glacier, for a total of about 16 hours in the St. Elias Range. John and Daniel graciously offered to fly out and help get me home, but I was confident I'd be alright, so I told them to stay and go climbing.

This accident has undoubtedly made me more wary of glacier travel, even though it's something I've been doing very regularly for over 15 years. I'm sure I will continue to do some occasional solo travel on glaciers, but I absolutely view solo glacier travel much more seriously now.

Analysis

This crevasse fall is what I consider to be my fifth close call in the mountains. I'm fortunate to have come away mostly unscathed every time, but if I'm not taking away injuries, hopefully I am at least taking away lessons:

1. *Climate and snowpack play huge roles in crevasse hazard.* The area of the St. Elias where we were is dry. We arrived at the start of April, and the snowpack in our base camp was a mere meter of dry, light snow. I think that glaciers like this (with a huge amount of ice below the firn line, in the ablation zone) generally exist in places that are cold enough to sustain large glaciers, but with low accumulation rates.

The crevasse that I fell into was at least two meters wide, and the bridge across it was never thicker than 40cm across the entire gap. This wide, super-thin snow bridge was not sagging even the tiniest amount, which is why I didn't have any clue it was there. Such a thin snow bridge, likely formed during a snowstorm many weeks earlier, didn't sag at all because it was in such a cold, dry environment, especially during the winter. In the Cascades, Chamonix, or the Coast Range, a snow bridge of those dimensions undoubtedly would have been sagging, and it would've been obvious a crevasse was there.

Basically, I have realized from this incident that crevasse hazard is much, much higher in relatively dry glaciated environments because the snow bridges are often very weak and very well hidden.

2. *Skis are a mixed blessing.* Most of us have been taught that having skis on your feet makes glacier travel safer, and

[This page] The thinly bridged crevasse in the St. Elias Range into which Colin Haley fell. *John Frieh*

there's no doubt this is generally true. However, I think my crevasse incident would've been avoided completely if I hadn't been wearing skis. If I had been on foot, then the moment I stepped off the solid ice I would've punched a leg through the edge of the snow bridge (something I have done many, many times before), and most likely I wouldn't have fallen in. Because I had skis on, I was able to ski well past the edge of the solid ice, and I didn't break through the snow bridge until I was in the middle of it. In other words, if you have skis on you're less likely to break through a snow bridge than when you are on foot, but you're more likely to break through the snow bridge completely (a proper crevasse fall) if you break through at all.

3. *A partner is a good idea.* This one's a no-brainer, but still worth mentioning. My crevasse accident is a perfect example of how much safety a climbing partner can provide compared to solo glacier travel, even if you aren't roped up.

4. *Wear your harness.* This accident has shown me that even if you are unroped having your harness on makes your ability to deal with a crevasse fall much better. In my case, it was very difficult to get to a position where I could put my harness on, and I was lucky that it was possible at all—and that was with only minor injuries.

5. *Use your umbilicals.* I have often used my ice-tool umbilicals while walking on glaciers, and this accident has confirmed to me that it is a good idea. Anytime you are in a crevasse, your ice tools will be very useful to you, and if you happen to be by yourself, ice tools provide your only significant chance of self-rescue (aside from perhaps aiding off of ice screws). During my crevasse fall I completely dropped both of my ski poles despite having the wrist loops on. I think the chance of dropping your ice tools during a crevasse fall is really high, and using umbilicals will make you much more likely to still have the ice tools when you stop falling.

6. *Use your crampons.* Like choosing whether to wear skis or not, realistically we will all decide whether to wear crampons depending on the snow conditions. If I had been wearing crampons when I fell in the crevasse, the chance of breaking

my ankles might have been higher, but this incident has made me realize how advantageous it would have been to have them on my feet already. If not on your feet, your crampons should be at the very top of your backpack, not buried in the bottom. Also, it goes without saying that you should ALWAYS have your crampons adjusted to your boots before you leave home, since many of us switch between different pairs of boots. Don't just throw them in your pack and plan to adjust them in the bottom of a crevasse!

7. *Technical climbing skills are useful.* I have always felt that being an experienced technical climber would be advantageous in a crevasse fall scenario, and this incident confirms that theory for me. If you are roped up, I have no doubt that a strong technical climber will be much faster and more competent at simply prusiking up a skinny rope (especially if he/she has any broken limbs). And obviously if you are by yourself, then being able to solo vertical ice is pretty much your only chance of getting out.

An important disclaimer: Any unroped crevasse fall is really, really sketchy and not a good idea! It is obviously most prudent to follow the advice I learned from the Mountaineers at age 14, and simply always be roped up on every glacier. I wanted to share my conclusions because I know there are many people, such as myself, who travel on glaciers unroped at times, and you won't be taught some of these conclusions during a typical glacier travel course. (Source: Colin Haley.)

FALL ON SNOW
Mt. McKinley, Denali Pass

On May 28 a team of five Polish climbers fell while descending the upper mountain above Denali Pass. They descended on their own power to the 17,200-foot camp on the West Buttress route and contacted an NPS ranger patrol there. One climber (39) reported a lower-leg injury and that she had trouble walking. Another (37) reported an arm injury and said the team was worried about continuing to descend unassisted.

One NPS team assisted the injured climbers down the ridge to the top of the fixed lines and then passed them off to another NPS team, who lowered them down the lines and helped them back to the 14,200-foot camp. The climbers waited for the rest of their team to descend from high camp, and then they all continued their descent unassisted.

Analysis

Because of language difficulties, the reason why all five fell is not known. It is known that one of the members had done some significant climbs, but the others only listed a few treks and an ascent of Mt. Elbrus. (Source: Jed Williamson.)

(Editor's note: We have been informed that Denali National Park rangers, per instruction from higher-ups, will no longer be providing analyses of climbing incidents in the park. This is unfortunate for the larger climbing community, because we will no longer have the benefit of their considerable knowledge and experience.)

HAPE
Mt. McKinley, West Buttress

On June 2, a client (43) on a guided trip was evacuated with a severe case of high-altitude pulmonary edema (HAPE). The guides had contacted rangers about one of their clients who seemed to be exhibiting signs and symptoms of HAPE. Rangers conducted an evaluation and agreed that the patient appeared to be exhibiting early signs of HAPE. The patient was left in the care of his team members, who claimed they had the knowledge and supplies to treat him appropriately.

Later in the day, the ranger patrol stopped back by the team's camp to check on the status of the patient. The guide team reported that the patient was in his tent and had been asleep for several hours. The ranger tried to communicate with the climber from outside of his tent, but he did not respond. Rangers opened the tent door and found him to be unconscious, unresponsive, and frothing from the mouth. The ranger team immediately put him on oxygen and treated him with altitude-illness medications. He eventually regained consciousness and mobility, and was evacuated from the 14,200-foot camp via the NPS helicopter. (Source: David Weber, Mountaineering Ranger.)

(*Editor's note: Both HAPE and HACE (high-altitude cerebral edema) are life-threatening conditions. A patient suspected of having either condition should be continuously monitored by someone with appropriate medical training.*)

FALL ON SNOW
Mt. McKinley, West Buttress

About 5 p.m. on June 23, a female client (28) on the AMS-Hamill expedition fell while negotiating the bergschrund at the base of the fixed lines at 15,400 feet on Denali's West Buttress route. At the time of the fall, her left arm was wrapped around the fixed line, which resulted in distal radius and ulna fractures. The bergschrund at this location created a step ranging from three to six feet throughout the climbing season. (Source: David Weber, Mountaineering Ranger.)

FALL ON SNOW – PULLED OFF BY TEAMMATES
Mt. McKinley, West Buttress

On July 7, Lilia Telenkevic (46), an experienced client on the Mt-19-7 Summits expedition, was pulled off her feet by her rope team while descending below the fixed lines, at around 15,000 feet, on the West Buttress route. During the fall she twisted her left knee.

NPS personnel at the 14,200-foot camp were notified on July 8 and assessed Telenkevic's injury. Medical assessment confirmed the victim's leg was non-weight bearing, and due to the increased risk of a ground evacuation a helicopter evacuation was initiated. Due to poor weather, evacuation was delayed until July 11, when the NPS helicopter 3AE evacuated Telenkevic to base camp, where she was transferred to a fixed-wing aircraft and transported to Talkeetna. (Sources: Tucker Chenoweth, NPS Ranger, and *Anchorage Daily News*.)

(Editor's note: 2013 was a year of few actual climbing incidents on Mt. McKinley, despite the fact that a record number of climbers summited last season: 787 (including a 78-year-old Alaskan man) out of the 1,151 registered. This was the lowest number registered since 1997. The number of climbers summiting McKinley has topped 700 in only four other years. The success rate was attributed to favorable weather conditions.

Non-climbing-related cardiac and spontaneous pneumothorax incidents also were reported but are not counted as accidents for our statistical tables.)

CALIFORNIA

PUNCH THROUGH SNOW, LEG STUCK
Mt. Shasta, Green Butte/Sargents Ridge

On January 20, Ranger Nick Meyers was notified by Siskiyou County SAR of an injured solo climber, Aaron Pessah (25), on the Green Butte/Sargents Ridge route at 11,300 feet. He was apparently unable to walk or descend due to a knee and leg injury. Meyers responded to Bunny Flat with USFS snowmobiles and California Highway Patrol helicopter H-16. He arrived at 11,300 feet, placed the climber in a screamer suit, and commenced a hoist at 4:30 p.m. Meyers carried the climber's gear down the mountain and returned to Bunny Flat by sundown.

Analysis

Aaron Pessah had moderate mountaineering experience and was climbing solo with a pack that weighed approximately 60 to 70 pounds. While he had all the best and latest gear, he also had way too much of it. Even for an experienced climber, attempting the Green Butte/Sargents route with a pack that heavy and awkward would be very difficult. (His plan was to do a four-day climb of Shasta. Most folks, even novice climbers, take two days.)

Pessah's injury occurred when his leg punched through the snow and down into a hole between some rocks. His large pack then threw him off balance, and his leg was tweaked because it was stuck in the hole. The location of his accident was before much of the technical climbing on that route, which was probably a good thing. (Source: Nick Meyers, USFS Lead Climbing Ranger and Avalanche Specialist.)

LOSS OF CONTROL – VOLUNTARY GLISSADE
Mt. Shasta, Cascade Gulch

On February 18 at 11:30 a.m., dispatch informed me (Celeste Fowler) of an overdue climber, J. Scherer (31), on Mt. Shasta. The reporting party was B. Thompson.

Thompson gave the following account. On February 17, he and Scherer began to climb Mt. Shasta. As they were descending by glissade, Scherer slid out of control for about 600 feet. He injured his ribs. Scherer was a medical student and knew he was not injured seriously. He did, however, complain of pain and wanted to descend rapidly to the vehicle at Bunny Flat. Thompson and

Scherer separated near Hidden Valley around 5:30 p.m. Scherer headed toward the vehicle, and Thompson went to pack up their camp from the night before and then head to Bunny Flat. Scherer was not at their car when he arrived. Thompson waited and then called a cab and went to the Alpine Motel for the night. He knew Scherer had enough supplies for the night. When he had not heard from Scherer the next morning, Thompson called 911.

The weather forecast showed a storm headed toward Mt. Shasta. A SAR team was deployed, and a request was made to California Highway Patrol Air Ops to respond. At 1:30 p.m. they had a visual on Scherer in the lower Cascade Gulch area. They set down and made contact with Scherer, loaded him, and transported him to Bunny Flat. Scherer had visible injuries to his face (abrasions) and still complained of rib pain, but declined medical attention. He said he became lost after he and Thompson separated. He described himself as a beginner climber. (Source: Nick Meyers, USFS Lead Climbing Ranger and Avalanche Specialist.)

LOSS OF CONTROL – VOLUNTARY GLISSADE
Mt. Shasta, Avalanche Gulch, Near "The Heart"

On June 16, a climber (33) was glissading on the Avalanche Gulch route at approximately 11,700 feet when he lost control and injured his shoulder. Apparently he had had surgery on the shoulder in the past and was familiar with the injury. The climber was in the process of self-rescuing when he was contacted by Ranger Brett Wagenheim, who performed a patient assessment. The climber declined further assistance. (Source: Nick Meyers, USFS Lead Climbing Ranger and Avalanche Specialist.)

(Editor's note: These two glissading incidents point to the importance of the techniques discussed in the Know the Ropes section of this edition. Climbers and hikers frequently overestimate their ability to control a glissade on icy or hard-packed snow.)

FALLING ICE
Mt. Shasta, Avalanche Gulch

On June 27, James Brown (30s), a Sierra Wilderness Seminars (SWS) guide, was struck by a large ice boulder in the lower leg and knocked off his feet. Ranger Nick Meyers was notified by SWS's Dave Cressman about 8:15 a.m. Cressman stated that Brown could not walk and potentially had broken his leg/ankle and needed a helicopter. Meyers called Siskiyou County SAR and, with proper approval, ordered a helicopter. Meanwhile, a couple of other guides were able to assist Brown down to Lake Helen from his initial accident location. A California Highway Patrol helicopter arrived shortly after the request and was able to pick up Brown at Lake Helen.

FALL INTO CREVASSE – INJURED LEG FROM JUMPING OVER CREVASSE
Mt. Shasta, Hotlum Glacier

On June 30, the U.S. Marine Corps Mountain Warfare Training Center out of Bridgeport was on Mt. Shasta conducting training exercises when Seargent Ruiz

(25) attempted to jump over a crevasse at around 11,500 feet. Upon landing on the other side of the crevasse, he injured his knee and fell back into the crevasse. The other Marines were able to rescue him from the crevasse and lower him to a place where he could be hoisted into a California Highway Patrol helicopter. (Source: Edited from information compiled and written by Nick Meyers, USFS Lead Climbing Ranger and Avalanche Specialist.)

INADEQUATE PROTECTION – MISPERCEPTION OF DIFFICULTY
Yosemite National Park, Half Dome

On May 13, Peter (31) and Alain (26), both from France, were climbing pitch six of the Regular Northwest Face (VI 5.9 C1), hauling a bag for a bivouac at Big Sandy Ledge. Peter took a 20-foot lead fall on the crack labeled "5.9 polished fingers" in the Supertopo guidebook. One piece of protection pulled and he landed on a ledge, injuring his ankle. They rapped to the base and called 911. They bivouacked that night, and the next day Peter was assisted by SAR team members to hike up to the main hiking trail on Half Dome. From there the NPS gave him a horse ride out due to his sprained ankle.

Analysis

Peter said that he misjudged the difficulty and the amount of protection needed to avoid the ledge. He rates himself as a 5.13 climber, but he fell on a 5.9 section. This is a good reminder that ratings are subjective, and that Yosemite crack climbing is a specialized technique. (Source: John Dill, NPS Ranger.)

INADEQUATE PROTECTION, PULLED OFF ROCK BLOCK, FALL ON ROCK, ROCK SEVERED ROPE
Yosemite National Park, El Capitan, Muir Wall

On the morning of May 19, Mason Robison (38) was killed in a fall while leading pitch 27 of the Muir Wall (VI 5.9 A2) on El Capitan. This pitch, rated C1, heads up a left-facing dihedral for 20 feet, traverses left around a small roof, and then continues up the dihedral. After placing three cams for aid above the belay, Robison placed a fourth behind a large, hanging block directly below the roof. As soon as he weighted the cam the block fell out. His belayer, Marc Venery (48), saw Robison fall backward past the belay and out of sight below, with "a big piece of rock in his lap." As the lead rope (10.5mm) began to tighten, it suddenly recoiled upward, completely slack. Venery knew immediately that it had been severed. In his words, "The haul line and tag line started whistling and whipping off the belay. I was in disbelief during those few seconds before they became tight."

Robison continued falling to the end of his haul line (a static 70m x 9.5mm), a total of 250 feet, including the lead fall above the belay. The haul line was fixed to the leftmost bolt of the anchor, and the rest of the anchor did not share the impact. Venery stated, "When...I reached over to pull on the lines that were still attached to Mason after he fell...the haul line was tight and fully weighted."

[This page] The roof on pitch 27 of the Muir Wall with the loose block (left) and the same spot after the block fell out. *Supertopo.com*

Venery shouted to Robison several times; when he heard no reply he began yelling for help. Yosemite Dispatch received reports of the incident immediately, and the NPS mobilized a response. From the Valley floor, rangers with a telescope could see Robison hanging in space, upright and motionless on the end of the haul line, a full rope length below Venery. Rescuers were lowered to Robison from the top of El Capitan and confirmed that he was dead.

Analysis

Recognizing and avoiding the risk: Robison was a very experienced climber, including previous El Cap routes. He and Venery were taking their time. They had added a rest day and had plenty of supplies, so haste was not an obvious factor. It appears that he simply thought the block was well attached. However, any hanging block or flake is risky, and you seldom know its strength or stability until it's too late. Furthermore, almost any protection becomes a lever when weighted, so it is a good idea to avoid potentially insecure features altogether.

Other climbers had skirted this block by traversing left below it to a vertical crack, but it is often difficult or impossible to navigate around hanging blocks or flakes. If it isn't possible to climb around the hazard, a pendulum may allow you to reach another climbable section of rock. Having enough specialized aid equipment and a bolt kit gives you other options, but in some situations retreat may be the best choice.

Rope damage from leader-induced rock fall: Robison's severed rope was not a fluke. A rope was cut in 2012 in Yosemite (the climber survived because he was leading on two ropes); another was cut in 2011 (fatal); and another was partially cut in 2010 (the leader was caught by the remaining core strands). Even if the rope survives, the falling rock may cause injury directly. When airborne with a rock in your lap, push it away if possible, but Fate may have other plans.

Surviving the fall: During the recovery and investigation, rangers noted that Robison's haul line was attached to a gear loop on the front of his chest harness by a locking carabiner. The gate of the carabiner was open and was also hooked onto the structural webbing of the chest harness. The chest harness had been pulled tightly around his chest and up under his arms, apparently by the force of the fall. Venery's photos of Robison leading previous pitches of the climb show the haul line attached to his seat harness. It is possible, but not likely, that the haul line became unclipped from the seat harness and reattached to the chest harness during the fall. A more plausible explanation is that he temporarily clipped the line to his chest loop during the belay changeover and then forgot to transfer it to the haul loop.

Robison died from severe trauma to his chest and fractures to the base of his skull. While impacts with the cliff may have contributed, the injuries are consistent with the chest harness constricting and crushing his chest. A 250-foot fall onto a static line is extremely risky in any event, but if the line had been attached to the full-strength haul loop on his seat harness—the recommended method and Robison's usual practice—the force might have been distributed more favorably.

After this incident some climbers recommended using a dynamic rope for a haul line, but this may not increase the overall safety of wall climbing. It is hard enough to free a hung-up haul bag with a static line, and harder still with a lead rope. Working harder to haul and descending more often to free bags could cause other problems, such as getting behind schedule, running out of water, becoming exhausted, and perhaps damaging a rope that has lower abrasion resistance. Hauling with a dynamic rope would result in a "softer" fall in the event that the lead line was severed, but this would require having a back-up rope. (Source: Jesse McGahey, NPS Ranger.)

FALLING ROCK – BELAYER STRUCK
Yosemite National Park, El Capitan, East Buttress

On June 2, British climbers Felix Kiernan (28) and Luke Jones (27) began an ascent of the East Buttress of El Capitan (5.10b). There was one rope team ahead of them, but because the British party was moving faster, the other team let them pass at the second belay. Jones describes what happened next: "Now, with the route free in front, Felix and I started moving at our own pace, and we were soon at the belay stance between pitches five and six. It was my turn to lead, so I took the rack, had a last look at the guidebook, and set off, all the while Felix bantering away in his poor attempt at a northern accent."

Based on later investigation, Jones was actually leading Supertopo pitch seven, not pitch six. In his words, "I had climbed up about 25 meters from the belay and was moving rightward along a small ledge. I then had to move around a bulge, and as I made the move the block I was standing on (about two feet by one foot) detached from the face, which caused me to fall about three feet onto the ledge. I shouted, 'BELOW!' as soon as I felt the block go, as is normal when the lead climber dislodges or drops anything. I looked down to check that Felix was okay, but saw that he was hanging upside-down from the belay. It was immediately apparent that the block had hit him and he was seemingly unconscious."

At 1:50 p.m., Yosemite's Emergency Communication Center received a 911 call from Robert Pressly and Parrish Berquist, the team that Kiernan and Jones had passed. Pressly and Berquist reported that a climber was hanging upside-down and unresponsive near pitch six of the East Buttress. Berquist climbed up to Kiernan while Jones built an anchor to rappel down to the belay. When Berquist arrived, at about 2:30 p.m., Kiernan appeared to be still breathing. She attempted but was unable to move him into an upright position, due to his awkward position and location. Eventually, Jones and Pressly also arrived at the anchor, but the group was still unable to help Kiernan. They initially thought he had a faint pulse, but ultimately they could not detect a pulse or breathing. They waited for rescuers to arrive. Shortly after 4 p.m., the climbing rescue team reached Kiernan and confirmed that he had no signs of life.

At around 6:30 p.m., Kiernan's body was extricated via helicopter long-line. The rescuers rappelled to the ground with Pressly, Jones, and Berquist.

Analysis

Despite Yosemite's reputation for solid rock, the risk of rockfall is ever-present. Here are some strategies for reducing that hazard:

1. *Wear your helmet.* Kiernan was wearing his, but we speculate that he leaned into the wall and ducked his head when he heard Jones yell. This is a logical action, and perhaps the only reasonable tactic at that time, but it put the unprotected part of his skull in perfect position for the fatal blow.

2. *Stay on route whenever possible.* The traveled route is often the most solid one, though rarely free of risk.

3. *Belayers*: Look at the pitch ahead, identify your escape options before the leader starts climbing, and keep an eye on the leader as much as possible. If you hear the leader's warning or the sound of rockfall and think you have time, a quick glance upward at the path of the rock may tell you whether to move or stay put—or you may get that rock in your face. That's why the sooner the leader yells a warning, the better your chance of avoiding injury. Given the short pitch, Kiernan may have had no time to decide, so he simply took the quickest course of action.

4. *Leaders*: Know when you are on loose rock. It will often have a hollow or ringing sound when knocked on, and may look cracked or detached. If those clues are present and there's no way to avoid it, first warn your belayer, then be gentle, pull down (not out), avoid lever points, avoid placing protection near the block, and consider retreat. And if your tactics fail and rock falls, yell immediately. (Sources: Luke Jones and Ben Doyle, NPS Ranger.)

FALL ON ROCK, INADEQUATE PROTECTION – MISPERCEPTION
Yosemite National Park, Leaning Tower, West Face

On June 24, Australian climber Shane Houbart (29) was on his second day of attempting to solo the West Face of Leaning Tower (Grade V 5.7 C2). After lunch at Ahwahnee Ledge, he began aiding up and right on pitch five. Shane had consciously decided to "run it out," judging that the steepness of the route would protect him from injuries if he fell. He left four pieces as fall protection and back-cleaned several others along the way. Then he placed a cam and bounce-tested it, but as he stepped higher in his aider the cam pulled and he fell about 50 feet. He pulled at least one more piece during the fall and struck a small ledge before a small nut held and he was caught by his Grigri. During the impact he felt a carabiner on his rack wedge deep into one side of his lower back.

After considerable effort and some problem-solving, he was able to transfer his weight onto his haul line, which was secured to the anchor at Ahwahnee Ledge—now above him—and ascend that rope to the anchor. By this time it was late in the afternoon. His injuries seemed limited to the lumbar-spine area and hip, but the pain was getting worse, so he decided to wait overnight before making a plan.

By morning the pain had increased, severely limiting his mobility. Shane could barely stand up, and he realized that he couldn't safely descend the route on his own, so he called 911. NPS rangers were short-hauled with the park helicopter to the top of Leaning Tower while other rescuers climbed up to him from the bottom. Using ropes rigged from the summit, the team lowered Shane to the ground.

Fortunately, Shane had not broken his back but was diagnosed with deep lumbar bruising. He has fully recovered and has since returned to successfully solo the route.

Analysis

Although this was his first attempt to solo a wall, Shane was an experienced wall climber, having done several Grade V and VI ascents in the Valley. He is not the first person to be injured on this pitch. In 2011 a climber took a long fall, breaking his patella and significantly injuring ligaments and tendons in his knee. In both cases the leader had back-cleaned several placements. Shane said he weighed the consequences of running it out, and as he led the pitch he looked at fall potential several times. He thought the pitch was so steep he couldn't possibly hit anything. Indeed, you might not hit during the free-fall phase, but as the rope arrests the fall, you may swing with considerable speed, usually toward the wall. Broken ankles or heels on overhanging sport climbs are surprisingly frequent for this reason. As a solo climber, the consequences of accidents are exacerbated since you have no one to help you retreat. (Sources: Shane Houbart and Jesse McGahey, NPS Ranger.)

STRANDED, RAPPEL ERROR – FORGOT TO UNTIE KNOT
Yosemite National Park, Royal Arches

On July 26, Ted (25) and Stephanie (23) climbed Royal Arches (Grade III 5.7 A0). They started at 10:30 a.m. Ted, with 4.5 years of experience versus Stephanie's one year, was the team leader. The climb took a lot longer than they expected, so they didn't begin the rappels until 1 a.m. on the 27th. They were climbing with one 60-meter rope, and when Ted set up the first rappel he tied knots in the ends of the rope. At the bottom of the first rappel, they pulled the rope, forgetting to untie the knot in the end they released. The knot got stuck in the anchor above. Ted thought about trying to ascend the stuck rope while tied to the end they still had, but the terrain between him and the anchor above looked like a "5.14 slab," it was dark, and even with their headlamps there were no visible opportunities for protection. The summer night was relatively warm and they each had a shell jacket, so they decided it was safest to wait until morning and then call for help. At 6 a.m. Ted called 911. Rescuers climbed the route and rappelled with Ted and Stephanie to the ground.

Analysis

Ted and Stephanie made the common mistake of getting a late start on an "easy" but long multi-pitch climb. Climbers who know the Royal Arches well often complete the route in eight hours or less. However, the climb involves 15 pitches of complex routefinding, a pendulum maneuver, and several traverses. As a result, parties with limited trad experience are frequently benighted. Starting early gives you more daylight to deal with potential snafus such as the dreaded knot jam, and there may even be another party above to drop your stuck rope to you. Finally, the more mentally and physically tired you are, the more likely you are to make mistakes. (Source: Ted and Jesse McGahey, NPS Ranger.)

STRANDED – NEW AND UNEXPECTED SITUATION, EXCEEDING ABILITIES
Yosemite National Park, Lambert Dome, Northwest Books

On August 2, Carl and Michelle (both from Canada) climbed Northwest Books (5.6). The descent is second- or third-class, but they found themselves on some slabs that Michelle was afraid to cross, despite her 5.7 climbing ability. Carl built a rappel anchor, but by this time, per Carl, Michelle was "freaked out": frozen with fear and unwilling to go back, ascend, or rappel to ledges below. They had food, water, two 60-meter ropes, and one headlamp. The sun was setting, so they called for help. SAR team members hiked to the summit, built belay anchors, descended to the party, and then guided them to the summit and the trail. (Source: John Dill, NPS Ranger.)

INADEQUATE WATER, FATIGUE, UNFAMILIAR WITH DESCENT
Yosemite National Park, Royal Arches, North Dome Gully

On August 13, Mike (21) and Russell (19) climbed Royal Arches (15 pitches, 5.7 A0). They finished late in the day, hiked along the rim to Washington Column, and began their descent via the North Dome Gully climbers' trail shortly before dusk. By this time they were almost out of water and feeling dehydrated. Near the top of the gully they encountered a short, exposed, fourth- or fifth-class slab that gave them the impression they had lost the trail, so they called 911, reported their situation, and asked for advice.

At the ranger's suggestion, they retraced their steps to the top of the Column and then called again for directions. It appeared they had been on the correct descent, or close to it, but Mike was so fatigued from climbing all day and from lack of water that he was reluctant to cross the slab even with a belay. They had enough food and clothing for the night, so they agreed to bivouac on the summit. In the morning, two Yosemite SAR team members hiked up the gully, provided them with food and water, and guided them back to the valley floor. The descent required some short belays and rappels for safety. No medical care was necessary.

Analysis

Mike and Russell got their descent information from *Yosemite Valley Free Climbs* (Supertopo). In retrospect, Russell believes that trying to navigate North Dome Gully without prior experience was a mistake, a concern the guidebook emphasizes. They were wise to back off when fatigued and heading into night, since the gully is tricky all the way down, even when you are on route. Russell also speculates that it may have been easier and safer to descend the Royal Arches rappel route. However, these rappels have their own routefinding challenges, and mistakes come easily to tired or hurried rappellers. (*See previous report.*)

These climbers had headlamps and enough gear for a safe bivouac, but they did not have enough water for a long day of climbing and a tricky descent. Royal Arches faces south and 100° F temperatures are common in August; even cooler weather dries you out quickly while climbing. (Source: Ben Doyle, NPS Ranger.)

FALL ON ROCK – INADEQUATE PROTECTION, NO BELAY ANCHOR, OFF ROUTE, EXCEEDING ABILITIES
Yosemite National Park, Half Dome, (not quite) Snake Dike

Early in the morning of August 27, 2012, Sam (24) and I (Paige, 27) hiked from the Little Yosemite Valley campground to the southwest face of Half Dome, intent on climbing Snake Dike (5.7 R). We had chosen the route because of the easy grade; it appeared to be a multi-pitch climb that fit our skill levels and aspirations. (We had each trad climbed for a year or two and were fairly new leaders.) We had a topo of the climb but did not bring the approach directions, so we followed a social trail marked by small cairns. Sam felt he'd be able to recognize the route from photos he'd seen earlier, but when we reached the general area it was a lot harder to identify than expected.

We spotted features resembling those on the topo, with what looked like a bolt anchor above a shallow roof, and decided this was probably our climb. Because of some notable differences, we formed a retreat plan if Sam led up and decided it was the wrong route. It looked harder than what we were expecting, but we weren't familiar with Yosemite ratings so we started anyway. (Later we decided the "bolts" must have been sparkling crystals. We were way off route.)

We scrambled up an easy fourth- or fifth-class crack to a ledge where there was plenty of room for me to stand and flake out the rope. From the edge of the ledge, three feet behind me, the cliff dropped almost vertically for 20 to 30 feet to the ground.

The face above was steep and smooth, but a flake on the right offered an easy crack that ran 15 to 25 feet up to a shallow roof. The crack provided opportunities for an anchor. The week before, a friend had pointed out to me for the first time the importance of anchoring the belayer in exposed locations, so it crossed my mind now, but neither Sam nor I brought it up. My rationalizations included, "We have a minimal rack (intended for Snake Dike) and he's going to need all that gear to build the next anchor. This is a pretty big ledge, and the climb is supposed to be easy."

Sam breezed up the crack with no problem and placed a small cam under the roof. I should have asked him to place a piece or two in the crack below to protect both of us, but I did not. I did suggest he place a second piece at the roof, but he said, "There's no room," and I didn't push it.

Sam fell twice when he couldn't find a hold above the roof. The cam held each time, and I stopped him easily. I did not suggest he reset the protection after those falls. (Now I know that's what you should do.) I said, "I think you should come down so we can see if we're off route," and he said, "No, let me give it one more shot." After a minute of contemplation he said, "I just have to go for it."

On the third try he made a dynamic move over the roof, but fell again. He had gone higher than before, so he fell harder and the cam pulled. He tumbled onto the belay ledge and then rolled over the edge. Because there had been no protection, I had quite a bit of slack, but it ran out and the rope came tight before he hit the ground below. I instinctively tried to catch him and didn't react in time to let go, so I was pulled off the belay ledge headfirst.

I didn't think about anything except for the ground I could see coming at me (or vice versa), and I put my hands out and rolled. Luckily the landing was all fine grit with no big boulders to hit. I opened my eyes and got up on all fours. I saw some blood on the ground from my bloody nose and thought, "I'm not dead!"

Sam was sitting against the cliff 15 feet away with a bloody forehead and no helmet. He said, "My arm is broken. We need to get out of here now!" His helmet was cracked and had come off in the fall, so I put it back on his head. He kept repeating, "We have to go," and I worried he might have a concussion or worse.

I said, "Hold on a second, our water's up on the ledge." I started to climb up to where I'd belayed, and at that moment I realized that my left leg was not working properly. I heard a popping sound whenever I attempted to move it. "My leg is broken. I can't get the water," I said.

I had no pain at that point, but very soon moving became a lot harder and my left leg wouldn't support my weight. I helped Sam get up and said, "I may not be able to walk," and he replied, "No, we gotta get out of here." He started walking fast and saying, "Come on, we gotta go." He was basically able-bodied except for his left arm. So I followed, hobbling and trying to pace myself. We had landed near a little social trail that headed down toward the main trail, about two miles away, where we were sure to find hikers. We had no cell phone.

When I realized our escape was going to take hours, I started yelling, but then I discovered there was something wrong with my lungs. While I could talk normally, there was no force to my yells. We only walked for a few minutes, maybe 200 yards. I didn't try to keep up, and when the terrain was rough I butt-scooted along. That's when I realized my right wrist was broken. Sam was about 100 yards ahead of me, out of sight and going about twice my pace, when he ran into two climbers headed for the real Snake Dike, which turned out to be a few hundred yards west of our route. I heard Sam using their cell phone to report to the rangers, so I just sat down, figuring that now I wouldn't have to crawl out of there. Soon, however, I realized that the rangers were coming to meet us on foot, because they had gotten the impression that the incident had been minor and we were going to walk out, which I doubted.

The two climbers came up and helped me continue to where Sam was. About an hour after Sam's call we called SAR back so I could give them my status. At their direction, I palpated my neck, which was sore. We had trouble figuring out my pain level because I didn't really have much unless I palpated an area, even when I weighted my leg. But after they got a clearer picture of what had happened, and more details about my condition, they told me that we could have neck and back injuries and that they were sending a helicopter. The two other climbers put out a bright yellow shirt to guide the aircraft while I tried to relax.

Two rangers were short-hauled to us. They decided that I needed to be immobilized in a litter and short-hauled out. Sam was short-hauled on the flight after mine, but he didn't require a litter. In the Valley I was transferred to an air ambulance and taken to a hospital in Modesto.

Sam had dislocated his elbow. Here is my diagnosis: left hip socket (pelvis) fractured though not displaced, symphisis pubis (pelvis) fractured and minimally displaced, right wrist fractured, six to eight ribs fractured, and the spinous processes on two neck vertebrae (C6 and C7) fractured. I also had a 20 percent right-side pneumothorax and a lacerated/bleeding liver, in addition to some lesser injuries. After lots of physical therapy, everything seems to have healed OK. I'm gym climbing again and recently ran a half-marathon. And I think Sam and I are a little wiser.

Analysis

Finding the route: In Yosemite there's a "corner with a crack that leads to a roof" everywhere you look. Unless you want to explore, and you have the skills and experience to do so, bring all the navigation tools you can, including photos, topos, and maps. If you load files onto your smartphone or camera, be sure you can see sufficient detail—that's been a problem in some cases. A paper copy for each member of your party never hurts, and everyone should know the descent/ escape route in case your team's leader is the one injured.

Under-protecting: Judge the hazard and the protection requirements based on what you see, even though you think you're on route and "the climb is supposed to be easy," and take a conservative approach to risk. This applies to everyone but is especially important for inexperienced parties who may not know enough to make informed decisions.

Communicating the hazard: Paige had concerns as soon as they reached the belay ledge, but she did not insist on an anchor, or at least on anchor-quality protection on the pitch. She also held back on saying something when Sam kept falling on that single cam. These can be uncomfortable social situations, and Sam was responsible for his own decisions, but being tied to him, Paige's life was also in his hands. A hesitation to communicate is often a factor in climbing accidents, as it is in many other fields.

Helmets: They're quite hard to crack. Sam's helmet may have prevented a debilitating or fatal injury.

After the fall: In a case like this the best action may be to stay put, given the risk of worsening a serious injury. But with no way to call for help, at least one of them had to move. (A whistle can be useful for raising the alarm.) When Sam finally contacted the NPS, his report was so mild (though unintentionally so) that it raised no concern and we directed nearby staff to meet them on foot. Yet Paige's internal injuries were quite close to being life-threatening and time-critical. Once we got a clearer picture of what had happened, we immediately shifted into high gear. Sam may not have understood the potential danger or how to give a clear report. One can learn about both of these topics in a Wilderness First Responder class. (Sources: Paige and John Dill, NPS Ranger.)

(*Editor's note: This narrative from 2012 did not appear in the last edition because of its length and a few missing details. The lessons illustrated are important enough to warrant inclusion this year.*)

NEAR MISS – ROPE-SOLOING WITH A STUCK ROPE THAT APPEARED TO BE FIXED
Yosemite National Park, Arch Rock

On December 3, I (Ryan, 31) went to Arch Rock to rope-solo fixed routes. I had heard there was a rope on Supplication (5.10c), and I had wanted to get on that route for more than a year. (*Note: Fixed-rope soling is free climbing while belayed by ascension devices connecting the climber to a fixed rope. It is a top-rope alternative that does not require a belayer.*)

The approach trail hits the base of the cliff near Midterm (5.10b). I hadn't planned on climbing Midterm, but I was excited to see a new-looking purple rope hanging down the route. There is a squeeze chimney toward the top of the climb, and chimneys being a weakness of mine, I decided I'd warm up on Midterm before heading over to Supplication.

I attached myself to the fixed line using a combination of a Petzl Mini-Traxion and a Petzl Basic Ascender, and started up Midterm. I immediately knew I was in for more than I'd bargained for. The 5.10b fingers start looked benign from the ground, but I ended up hanging on the rope several times in that section. I cruised through 40 feet of 5.9 hands before getting worked in the 5.10 offwidth section below the chimney (again hanging a few times). At a nice rest stance near the top of the offwidth (80 feet off the deck), I noticed that the rope did not, in fact, go to the top of the chimney, but ended about six feet above me in the entrance of the chimney. I thought that maybe it was fixed to a chockstone in the chimney, but I couldn't see it from my stance. Clearly, the rope-fixer had not been as excited as I was about getting chimney practice! Without climbing any farther, I popped my Grigri onto the rope, lowered myself to the ground, and had a snack. I did two laps on Supplication and gave Leanie Meanie a try (failed) before heading home for the day,

Once home, I went to Mountainproject.com to see what others thought of that fingers section on Midterm. On the Midterm webpage, I saw a comment from the day before from a guy who had gotten his purple rope stuck and was asking if someone would get it for him. My heart dropped. It took a few minutes to come to terms with the fact that I had been climbing and lowering on a stuck rope. Rain was coming in that night, so I hoped no one else would be up there for a few days. The next morning I told Ranger Jesse McGahey what had happened.

Analysis

Ryan: I use fixed ropes regularly to get laps in when I can't find partners. I set up my own fixed ropes for one-day use throughout the year, and in winter I climb other people's ropes at the Cookie and Arch Rock. Until Midterm, I had taken for granted that a rope with a coil at the bottom, hanging off the ground, was a fixed rope intended for climbing. Going forward, I will continue using other people's fixed ropes but will make sure I can clearly see the rope tied into an anchor above before climbing the route.

Jesse McGahey: On December 5 I climbed Midterm with a partner to retrieve the purple rope. About 85 feet up and 30 feet below the regular anchor, a single bight of the rope, four feet from its end, was pinched between the face of the chimney and a softball-size rock in some sand. It took two seconds to pull it out. The rope was stuck only six to eight feet above where Ryan had stopped. If he had continued climbing into the chimney, he would have changed the angle of pull on the rope, very likely pulling it out. He then effectively would have been free-soloing a 5.10 offwidth chimney.

The purple rope was a 9.4mm dynamic lead line, which might raise one's suspicions, since climbers usually leave static lines for fixed-rope soloing. While I was retrieving the rope, a climber came up to the base and told us not to take it down, that it was fixed, and that his friends had left it there. Even after we told him it was not fixed, he pleaded with us to leave it up so that he could take a lap on it. We possibly saved his life by removing the line.

In 2012 a climber became stranded on the Cookie Cliff after rope-soloing a fixed line (*Accidents 2013*). Stories of climbers incorrectly rigging their ascension/belay devices are common, including a 20-foot fall at the Cookie Cliff. Others have completed a pitch only to discover they've forgotten their descent device. Somehow none of these mishaps have involved injuries, but complacency abounds. As in other forms of climbing, fixed-rope climbers should be systematic and wary about their practices. (Sources: Ryan, a.k.a. "Mr. Lucky," and Jesse McGahey, NPS Ranger.)

(*Editor's note: Many of the names used in the reports from Yosemite are pseudonyms, used at the request of the climbers.*)

FALL ON ROCK, RAPPEL ERROR – INADEQUATE RAPPEL ANCHOR, FAILURE TO FOLLOW ROUTE
Sierra Nevada, Mt. Emerson

On July 6, a female climber (42) was seriously injured while descending the southeast face of Mt. Emerson (5.4). Sometime around 1 p.m. she fell approximately 100 feet down a wide, 85° chimney while she was rappelling off the route. A single nut or cam was used as the anchor and it failed. Falls of such a distance are often fatal, so she was fortunate to survive the accident. She sustained serious injuries, including a traumatic brain injury, broken pelvis, severely broken ankle, a broken jaw, a broken nose, and numerous deep lacerations. Her helmet was found broken into three pieces.

Hikers on the Piute Pass Trail heard screams coming from Mt. Emerson and reported the incident to the Inyo County Sheriff's Department. The victim's climbing partner was unable to rescue her friend, and the fallen climber was unable to rappel any further due to her injuries. The uninjured partner made the difficult decision to stabilize her and seek help. The victim was left alone approximately 200 feet above the base of the mountain, on a nearly vertical rock wall, in a very disoriented state.

Due to the life-threatening nature of the accident, Inyo County Sheriff's Office (ICSO) requested helicopter support from California Highway Patrol. The ICSO also requested support from Inyo County Search and Rescue (Inyo SAR). The pilot spotted the victim at approximately 5 p.m. and attempted to get close enough to the wall to lower a flight medic to her position. After several attempts, the pilot determined that he could not safely get close enough to lower the medic. Windy conditions and the steepness of the rock wall prevented the helicopter from accessing the victim's position.

Two Inyo SAR members hiked in and climbed 180 vertical feet up to the victim, reaching her position, near 11,700 feet, just before sunset. Her head injury made her extremely disoriented and uncooperative, and put her at risk of falling again due to the steep, precarious position she was in. She was safely anchored to the wall by the team leader and given a medical evaluation. A determination was made that her condition was serious and potentially life threatening.

Without any helicopter support, four more Inyo SAR members had to carry in over 200 pounds of medical and technical rescue gear. The Inyo SAR team of six volunteers initiated a two-line technical rescue, which enabled them to lower the patient on a backboard in a titanium litter down the steep rock face. Three SAR volunteers climbed to the patient while three remained on the ground. The transfer of the patient to the backboard and litter was complicated by the steep wall and the serious potential for rockfall. By this time, the patient's mental state was deteriorating and she was becoming combative, requiring additional restraints. The technical lower was a very complex operation due to her precarious position and sensitive medical condition. It was accomplished with the absolute minimum number of SAR personnel possible: two belayers and one litter attendant descending with the victim. The darkness, high elevation, loose rocks and vertical terrain, and the victim's mental state made it extremely challenging to facilitate a smooth rescue.

After the technical lower was finished at approximately 2:30 a.m., two SAR volunteers with EMT certification assessed the victim's condition. She was given supplemental oxygen, her broken ankle was stabilized, and her lacerations were treated. The victim was packaged for transport down the remainder of the mountain. The terrain below involved 500 vertical feet of loose rocks and talus slopes to the trail. Once the Piute Pass Trail was encountered, a wheel was attached to the bottom of the litter and the victim was transported over

1.75 miles of steep, rocky trail. She was lifted into an ambulance at sunrise, approximately 15 hours after the accident, and was hospitalized in Reno, Nevada. It was expected that she would eventually make a complete recovery.

Analysis

The southeast face of Mt. Emerson is an attractive route to beginning backcountry climbers. It is not far from the trailhead, appears to be easy (a 5.4 rating), and it is now in the High Sierra Supertopo guide. However, this route actually has two short sections lower on the face that are closer to 5.6 or 5.7. Higher up on the route, there is a lot of routefinding that is difficult to document on a topo.

This party apparently got lost higher on the face and decided to retreat. Their retreat involved downclimbing until they got to the higher of the harder sections. At this point, the patient decided that she did not feel secure downclimbing and asked to rappel. It is not clear why only one piece of gear was used to make an anchor. (The other climber was planning to clean the anchor and downclimb this section.) The anchor failed and the climber bounced down the chimney system that defines the lower portion of the climb.

Backcountry Sierra Nevada routes are rarely easy and require:
- Routefinding in complex terrain
- Building anchors in often less than perfect rock
- Climbing on less than perfect rock
- A high degree of self-reliance
- Someone in the front country must know what you are doing and when to call 911. (Source: Edited from a report by Julie Vargo, Ariana Wylie, and Paul Rasmussen, Inyo County Sheriff's Posse SAR.)

(*Editor's note: This narrative is included both for its climbing lessons and to provide the reader with an understanding of what may be required for a rescue.*)

HAPE
Sierra Nevada, Elinore Lake

Four intermediate mountaineers ascended the South Fork of Big Pine Creek on August 30 to do some alpine climbing. They camped at Elinore Lake (about 11,000 feet), and on August 31 they headed up Scimitar Pass with the intention of climbing Mt. Sill. One of the team members, Robert Gertz (28), mentioned feeling like "there was ice in my lungs." He reported no other symptoms. The group made it to about 13,200 feet and then turned around due to time constraints. That night they camped at Elinore Lake. Robert found it harder and harder to breathe as the night progressed and began coughing up brownish mucus.

After a sleepless night, team member Michael Colby hiked up to a high point where there was cell service and called 911. He informed the Inyo County Sheriff's Office of Robert's condition, and was told the party should help the patient descend and continue to monitor him. That day the group made it only two miles, and this took 10 hours as the patient's condition deteriorated.

Inyo County Search and Rescue was called to action early on the morning of September 2. Robert had reached a critical stage and could no longer move without extreme and dangerous effort.

Two rescuers started out immediately and requested helicopter assistance due to the patient's serious and worsening condition. A California Highway Patrol helicopter arrived soon afterward and searched for a landing zone while the rescue team, comprised of two Wilderness EMTs, assessed the patient. Robert was prone with his head elevated on a log. His blood pressure, heart rate, skin color, pupils, lung sounds, and level of consciousness were not alarming. However, he could not speak even a word without severe respiratory distress. No oxygen saturation measurement was obtained on scene. He was placed on 15 liters per minute of oxygen via a non-rebreather mask. Focus then shifted to the pending helicopter extraction.

The helicopter was able to land within 50 feet of the scene. Even so, in Robert's weakened state it took him about 15 minutes to walk to the helicopter, pausing and even sitting down to rest every few steps. The effort of stepping up into the cockpit was colossal for the patient. He was immediately flown to a rendezvous with an ambulance on the valley floor. In the ambulance, after descending to 4,000 feet and with at least 45 minutes of high-flow oxygen, his O2 saturation was still around 60 percent. (Normal O2 saturation levels are above 90 percent.) Robert was transported to Northern Inyo Hospital, where he was diagnosed with severe high altitude pulmonary edema (HAPE) and given treatment. He has since made a full recovery.

Analysis

What's striking about this accident is that, despite the team's substantial preparation and knowledge, little could have been done to prevent it. The party was experienced and had been climbing conservatively. They began descending immediately after the onset of symptoms and called 911 nearly as quickly. The patient pushed himself to his physical limit trying to get down. When he hit that limit, his friends pushed themselves to theirs in the attempt to help him. By the time rescuers found the group, Robert and his partners had given up hope of getting him out unassisted. The patient's pants were completely shredded from the waist to the knees from his struggle to descend over sharp talus after he could no longer walk. The rescue team and helicopter arrived just in time, and Robert's friends were truly heroic in their efforts to assist him to a lower elevation. (Source: Edited from a report by Julie Vargo, Ariana Wylie, and Paul Rasmussen, Inyo County Sheriff's Posse SAR.)

(Editor's note: This narrative is presented to remind us that AMS, HAPE, and HACE can happen at relatively low elevations and can be difficult to alleviate.)

INADEQUATE RAPPEL ANCHOR, FALL ON ROCK, FALLING ROCK
Joshua Tree National Park

On February 25, my daughter Helen (16) and I (47) attempted to find an area where I'd climbed the previous week, but we couldn't find it so we decided to climb a little crag that looked like mostly class four or easy class five. My limited previous lead climbing experience had been about 5.3, so this seemed like a safe

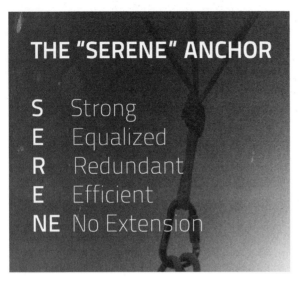

THE "SERENE" ANCHOR

S Strong

E Equalized

R Redundant

E Efficient

NE No Extension

climb within my ability. Both of us were wearing helmets. I led a low-angle slab about 10 feet tall. I built a redundant anchor out of two cams and belayed my daughter while she came up, then belayed her while she downclimbed.

Not wanting to leave my gear, I removed the cams and built a rappel anchor by inserting a rap ring into a piece of webbing tied around a peanut-shaped boulder about three feet long, sitting on a horizontal ledge with other rocks wedged in above it. The peanut seemed solid and resisted any attempts to budge it. Halfway down my 10-foot rap, as the angle of the slab got steeper, I heard the peanut start to move above me. I fell and the rock immediately hit me in the shoulder. I called down to my daughter that I was hurt. She ran to a park ranger who happened to be nearby and got him to come over. I was in almost no pain, but was unable to raise my right arm and believed I had a dislocated shoulder. The ranger helped me find an easy downclimb so I could get the rest of the way down one-handed. I drove home and went to the ER, where I learned that my clavicle had been broken into four pieces.

Analysis

This was a cheap lesson in how to make better climbing decisions, and I'm very glad that my daughter wasn't hurt. I knew the SERENE acronym, which would have told me not to rap from this anchor, but I didn't use it. Instead I used a heuristic mode of decision-making: I had recently seconded a bunch of trad climbs where the routine was to climb, clean pro, and then rap off, so I simply followed what had become my habit. Downclimbing would have been safer than rapping off this unreliable anchor. I am humbled and sobered by this accident and will hold myself to a more systematic, checklist-oriented approach in the future. (Source: Ben Crowell.)

FALL ON ROCK
Idyllwild, Tahquitz Rock, The Bat Crack

On May 17, Lucas Dunn (21) fell 300 feet to his death while rappelling from the top of the Bat Crack (5.11a), the first of four pitches on the Vampire (5.11a). According to Dunn's partner, Greg Davis, the fatal accident likely occurred due to rockfall encountered during the rappel. "I heard a crash and turned to see Lucas coming down the slab with a few giant rocks, possibly the loose one I [had] noted, and the rope," wrote Davis on Supertopo.com. "Once he passed the slab and rolled off the ledge system, I knew he was unconscious."

Davis was given a rope by two nearby climbers and was able to rappel the remaining 175 feet to reach Dunn while the other climbers called in the accident. Upon arrival, Davis noted that Dunn was still alive but unconscious. Despite being administered CPR, Dunn never regained consciousness. He was airlifted from Tahquitz in a helicopter. Davis wrote on Supertopo.com, "For those that didn't know him, he was 21 years old, 6 feet tall, bright, and one hell of a climber." To read Davis' very moving full account of the accident, search at Supertopo. (Source: Edited from reports on Supertopo.com and Mountainproject.com.)

COLORADO

AVALANCHE, HYPOTHERMIA – FATIGUE, EXCEEDING ABILITIES, FAILURE TO FOLLOW ROUTE
Rocky Mountain National Park, Ypsilon Mountain

David Laurienti (43) and Lisa Foster (45) were caught in an avalanche on the evening of March 17 while descending from Ypsilon Mountain (13,514 feet). The pair had departed from the Lawn Lakes trailhead at 3:15 a.m. on the morning of March 16 with the intent of climbing Ypsilon via the Blitzen Ridge route and descending Donner Ridge to the south. Blitzen Ridge is a technical mountaineering route (Grade II, 5.4 to 5.7) with numerous sections of fifth-class climbing.

The party arrived at the start of the crux technical section (the Four Aces) at approximately 9:45 a.m. They spent the rest of the day on the 16th negotiating this technical section in winter conditions, and finished the Fourth Ace around 7 p.m. Given that they were moving slower than anticipated, and with darkness imminent, they discussed descending a northeast-facing couloir just west of the Fourth Ace into the Fay Lakes drainage. They elected not to descend here due to concerns about avalanche conditions and wind loading in the couloir, and instead opted to continue toward the summit and less technical terrain.

They continued their ascent at 7:30 p.m. and climbed through the night of March 16, getting off route due to darkness. They veered into more technical terrain to the north of Blitzen Ridge, which further slowed their progress. By dawn of March 17, they were still making their way toward the summit. They crossed the Northeast Couloir, north of Blitzen Ridge, below the upper wind-loaded slopes, and climbed to a notch in the ridge about 200 vertical feet below the summit of Ypsilon Mountain around 5 p.m. on the 17th.

At their high point (13,300 feet), David was exhibiting obvious signs of fatigue and mild hypothermia. They discussed the hazardous avalanche conditions, but their predicament led them to conclude that descending the Northeast Couloir was the best option at the time. They began their retreat via that route. Because they had a 60-meter rope and a light alpine rack, they couldn't rappel all of the rocky technical terrain. The climbers stayed roped together, using their entire

[This page] Ypsilon Mountain, with Northeast Couloir marked. The Four Aces are the rock spires at left. *Brian Lazar/Colorado Avalanche Information Center*

length of rope. They simul-climbed down the right side of the couloir, with Lisa in the lead and placing rock protection into the adjacent rock face.

The pair was approximately halfway down the narrow portion of the couloir when a soft wind slab released above David. It is unclear whether he triggered the slide from below or if it released naturally from wind-loading, but given the start zone and the position of the climbers at the time of the avalanche, wind-loading was suspected. There were two pieces of protection in place (a nut and 0.75 Camalot) at this time. Both climbers took a violent fall of approximately 100 feet, hitting rocks and ice on the way down. The Camalot arrested their fall, with David coming to rest about 30 feet above Lisa. (The nut pulled loose and was dangling from the rope after the avalanche.) The majority of the avalanche debris ran by the climbers and cemented the rope into place, rendering it irretrievable. David indicated that he was not injured, but the coroner's report later indicated he had minor injuries. Lisa sustained broken ribs, a torn MCL, a broken coccyx, and damage to her wrist ligaments.

The two descended the lower portion of the couloir, with David walking in crampons and Lisa walking in crampons until she changed into snowshoes on the lower snow ramp. By this time darkness had fallen again. They walked approximately 1/4 mile from the bottom of the couloir. Lisa changed back to crampons to descend two small ice steps. They walked most of the way down a snow slope before David was no longer able to travel. His level of consciousness had begun to deteriorate rapidly during this quarter-mile walk. Lisa positioned

David in as sheltered and as comfortable position as possible, and then both of them spent the night on the snow slope. Lisa reported that David became unresponsive around 8:30 p.m.

Lisa departed the scene at dawn on the morning of March 18, and after walking a couple of miles she encountered National Park Service search and rescue members just above and northeast of Ypsilon Lake. Search and rescue provided emergency medical care and facilitated her transport back to the trailhead. NPS search and rescue members and a Colorado Avalanche Information Center forecaster went in to locate David on the morning of March 19, and found him on the snow slope beneath the ice steps. The official cause of death as determined by the coroner was hypothermia. Lisa's survival is impressive and improbable given the length of time exposed to brutal weather conditions and the extent of her injuries. (Source: Colorado Avalanche Information Center.)

Analysis

It seems that the biggest contributor to this fatality was not the avalanche per se, but the climbers' inability to traverse the technical portions of the ridge quickly enough. Blitzen Ridge is long even in ideal summer conditions, and in winter conditions it can be very committing. It would have been more prudent to descend, given the length of time it took the climbers to pass the Four Aces. Alternatively, if they were determined to summit, they should have carried bivy gear and a stove so that they could refuel, recharge, and summit and descend safely. (Source: Joe Forrester.)

FALL ON ROCK, FALLING ROCK
Rocky Mountain National Park, Longs Peak

On August 16, Christian Mason (34) took a roped fall of about 50 feet and suffered numerous injuries after being hit by falling rock while simul-climbing in the North Chimney (5.5), below the Diamond face. Rockfall reportedly hit him while he was in the lead. Fortunately, he was roped and did not fall to the base of the east face of Longs Peak.

Mason reported: "One of the hardest things for me has been not knowing what caused the accident. A falling rock knocking me out seems like the most logical explanation, but I really have no idea. I had always thought of myself as a safe and reasonably conservative alpine climber. I remember swapping leads with my partner about two-thirds of the way up the North Chimney. I remember placing the Camalot (#1) that I fell on and continuing up around 20 feet to another ledge. The rock quality was pretty poor there, and after looking at the potential fall I started looking for someplace solid enough to place reliable gear. That's my last clear memory. I can remember bits and pieces of the next three days, but it's very disjointed.

"I ended up with two skull fractures, six broken ribs, a broken left scapula, a broken neck (fracture of C1-2), and broken back (T5 and T6). Amazingly, I don't appear to have any nerve damage. While I'll have a fairly long recovery, I should be able to recover more or less fully."

After receiving the call for assistance, a park ranger/park medic climbed up the North Chimney and reached the climber at 11:30 a.m. while two additional rangers rappelled from Chasm View. Christian was evacuated with the help of Rocky Mountain National Park rangers and fellow climbers. (Source: Christian Mason.)

Analysis
The North Chimney is a ca. 450-foot, relatively low-angle approach to the vertical Diamond wall, with some loose rock (especially on the steepest section near the top) and low fifth-class climbing. Many climbers choose to solo the North Chimney approach. However, given the popularity of this route, climbers should take extra care to protect themselves from rockfall, especially if there are parties above. Christian's survival clearly demonstrates the value of roping up and placing protection in such an environment, even on technically easy terrain. (Source: Aram Attarian.)

FALL ON ROCK, PROTECTION PULLED OUT, INADEQUATE BELAY
Rocky Mountain National Park, Lumpy Ridge
On August 22, Corey Stewart (22) fell 30 feet while leading on Batman Pinnacle at Lumpy Ridge. CPR was begun minutes later by people at the scene, but they were unable to revive him. According to witnesses, Stewart fell off, some gear pulled out, he landed on and then went off the belay ledge, and the belayer was pulled off afterward. Due to severe thunderstorms, recovery efforts had to be postponed until the next day. (Source: NPS Morning Report.)

Analysis
This unfortunate incident might have been compounded if the belayer had been injured too. An appropriate anchor could have prevented both climbers from falling off the ledge. (Source: Aram Attarian.)

AVALANCHE – WEATHER, POOR POSITION
Rocky Mountain National Park, Dragon's Tail Spire
About 3 p.m. on November 21, two climbers were ascending Enter the Dragon (5.7 M4 Steep Snow) on the southeast aspect of Dragon's Tail Spire. The leader (Climber 1) was about 60 feet below a fixed anchor at the end of their third pitch when he triggered a small wind-slab avalanche on the snow slope above. Climber 1 just managed to stand his ground as the slab overran his position, and Climber 2 was not hit because he was protected by overhanging rock. Climber 1 finished the pitch and tied into a fixed anchor, and then brought Climber 2 up. The crown at the point of release measured eight inches, and the slab was approximately 60 by 60 feet. At this point, both climbers knew it was time to get off the route and they began rappelling down the route toward the Dragon's Tail Couloir.

By about 5:30 p.m., Climber 1 had rappelled relatively low into Dragon's Tail Couloir. After taking a few steps down the slope, he heard a noise like a freight train high in the couloir above. Climber 2 was still tied into a tree anchor above. Climber 1 looked up and saw a wall of white five to ten feet high come over a prominent rock band. Climber 1 buried his axe and his crampons and prepared for the hit. A half second later he was cartwheeling down the slope, engulfed by the slide. After fighting to stay on top, he popped to the surface after being carried nearly 500 feet. A few seconds later he heard another roar and was hit by another slab avalanche and carried farther down the couloir, but he was able to log-roll off this slab into a rocky shelter against the couloir's edge.

Climber 2 watched Climber 1's headlamp light disappear as he was carried down slope in this large, naturally triggered avalanche. After the slide stopped, Climber 2 waited for the second slide to run its course before rapping down to find Climber 1 dazed, hyperventilating, and coughing blood, but otherwise uninjured. Both climbers ascended the slope to retrieve their rope before descending and hiking out to their car. The avalanche debris was waist- to neck-deep and ran the width of the couloir. Among the debris, the climbers noted one-foot-thick chunks of wind slab in addition to wet storm slab, suggesting heavy wind-loading high on the southeast aspect of Flattop Mountain. (Source: Colorado Avalanche Information Center.)

[This page, top] Dragon's Tail Spire and the Dragon's Tail Couloir to its right. [This page, bottom] Crown of the small slab avalanche triggered on the third pitch of Enter the Dragon, prompting the climbers' retreat.

Analysis

The climbers knowingly chose to climb this route during a storm. Both climbers were adept in self-rescue and wilderness medicine, educated in avalanche safety, and familiar with the terrain at hand, having previously climbed the same route and other routes on the Flattop Mountain massif. On the day of the climb the avalanche danger scale read low to moderate for all aspects and elevations. A melt-freeze cycle the week prior had created excellent climbing conditions on route, and both climbers noted a consolidated, spring-like snowpack above tree line during their initial approach up the Dragon's Tail Couloir and on the first pitches of the climb. They did, however, underestimate the potential for wind loading caused by high winds during the previous days, which appeared to form thick wind slabs on top of the melt-freeze crust at higher elevations. On route, the climbers noted that it began to snow very hard around 2 p.m., with accumulation reaching nearly a foot by 5 p.m. Unusually for late November in the Colorado high country, the snow was wet and heavy. This rapid buildup of wet storm snow, coupled with dangerous wind-loading, conspired to create a perfect storm of deadly conditions for both human-triggered and natural avalanches.

The southeast aspect of Flattop Mountain, where these avalanches occurred, is ripe for similar avalanche events. Despite numerous avalanche accidents here, it remains one of the most popular winter playgrounds for skiers and climbers in all of RMNP. Climbers entering an alpine environment like this in winter should be able to identify avalanche terrain, be familiar with safe travel in avalanche terrain, have good decision-making and rescue skills, and carry the appropriate self-rescue equipment. Don't underestimate the rapid buildup of storm snow on steep slopes or become complacent with familiar terrain. (Sources: Climber 1 and Aram Attarian.)

FALL ON ROCK, BELAYER ERROR, INEXPERIENCE
Boulder Canyon

In July, Scott Jones (22) was dropped from the top of Iron Maiden (5.9) in Boulder Canyon by a belayer he had met through a climbing community web site. Scott describes the incident:

"I should establish that this was not a typical rapping/lowering miscommunication. I was the first to lead the route, and we established that he was going to lead it after I hung the draws." Before climbing, Scott also verified that the belayer had loaded his device, a Grigri, correctly. "When I reached the chains I yelled down, 'Take.' I didn't feel any pressure from the rope, so took both hands and grasped the line and began lowering myself. As I neared a bulge 10 feet below the chains, I felt (possibly mistakenly) the rope come tight." At this point, though he still could not see or hear the belayer, Scott assumed he was being lowered and let go of the rope. He fell about 60 feet to the ground.

"Luckily the initial bleeding wasn't too bad and I was able to self-rescue across the creek to the highway. A generous climber replaced my blood-drenched shirt with his own and offered to drive me to the hospital. Unfortunately, the traffic was bumper to bumper, but as luck would have it a man on a Harley was passing by, so I hopped on. I quickly made my way through traffic until I reached the cause of the backup and the hospital."

Analysis

"The next day I spoke to the belayer (if you can call him that) and was able to piece together what happened: He paid out slack at the top of the route by pulling on the Grigri's lever while letting go with his brake hand." The belayer must have held the Grigri too far open and lost control of the lower.

"I'm guessing the only thing that kept me from the morgue was the fact that the rope was hopelessly kinked, creating a good deal of friction. It may have also tangled itself below the Grigri just before I slammed into the ground. I guess the only advice I could give is not to be afraid to decline a belay from someone who gives you a bad feeling. I see now that a perceived insult is a much better outcome than a trip to the hospital." (Source: Scott Jones on Mountainproject. com.)

(Editor's note: "Blind date" partners are always a cause for extra caution. Make sure you and your partner fully understand each other's experience level, and visually verify the other climber's belay and lowering methods before starting to climb. A belayer must never let go of the rope with his brake hand even when using "assisted braking" devices such as the Grigri. See page 68 for more about belaying with a Grigri.)

FALL ON ROCK, PROTECTION PULLED OUT, INADEQUATE BELAY
Boulder Canyon

Late in the afternoon of August 22, two male climbers (both 24) fell approximately 70 feet while attempting the Spoils (5.12a/b) on Bell Buttress. The accident occurred after the leader rested on a piece of protection he had placed before the first bolt. The leader attempted the next move and came off, pulling the piece, and in the process pulled his unanchored belayer off a ledge. They both tumbled all the way into Boulder Creek.

Both climbers were conscious and breathing at the time of their rescue. They were transported to Boulder Community Hospital. (Source: Edited from a report at Mountainproject.com.)

Analysis

Many of the climbs on Bell Buttress start from a narrow ramp that traverses the cliff above a lower rock band. Although climbers often choose to belay with no bottom anchor on this ledge, this incident clearly demonstrates why a secure anchor must be established anytime the belay stance is exposed. (Source: Aram Attarian.)

FALL ON ROCK, PROTECTION PULLED OUT, NO HELMET
Boulder Canyon

On August 31 a woman (20) was seriously injured when she fell approximately 30 to 40 feet after a piece of gear pulled while she was climbing on the Happy Hour Crag. According to her belayer, she was somewhat run-out when she placed her third cam and made one or two more moves. She slipped and pulled out the last cam. The belayer tried to take in slack as quickly as he could. When he realized that she was going to hit the ground, he let go of the rope and tried to catch her. She suffered a broken neck and fractured skull. She was not wearing a helmet. (Source: Matt Cochran, via a series of posts on Mountainproject.com.)

Analysis

Run-outs are often a part of traditional climbing, with the risk of injury being greater when they occur near the ground. Climbers must stay aware of the consequences of any failure of climbing protection, and should consider backing up protection where failure could be catastrophic. While this fall still may have resulted in a head injury, climbing with a properly fitted helmet can help reduce the severity of an injury. (Source: Mark Vermeal.)

STRANDED – ROPE STUCK, DARKNESS, INADEQUATE CLOTHING
Boulder, Third Flatiron

During the early evening of January 26, three climbers (two males, one female) became stranded while climbing the Standard Direct (5.2) on the East Face of the Third Flatiron. The group had decided to descend from partway up the route and was preparing a rappel when their rope became stuck above them, stranding them 200 feet above the ground.

"After the rope got stuck we attempted to free it ourselves, and then asked for help from nearby climbers. When neither of those solutions worked, we discussed calling for help for probably 90 minutes," said one of the climbers. Rain started to fall, and despite being stuck 200 feet off the ground and not having appropriate clothing and equipment for the conditions, the climbers still delayed calling for help. They eventually called 911 and Rocky Mountain Rescue Group (RMRG) responded. Volunteer rescuers climbed above the stranded party on rain-soaked, slick rock, established lowering anchors, and used the anchors to assist the climbers to the ground.

Analysis

The stuck climbers were reasonably equipped to complete the climb—in daylight and with good weather. They were not prepared for complications such as a stuck rope, darkness, and deteriorating weather. First they attempted to solve the stuck rope problem themselves, and then they asked for assistance from nearby climbers. These were appropriate actions. However, even if self-rescue is being attempted, Rocky Mountain Rescue Group (RMRG) encourages calling for help early. If the problem is solved before RMRG arrives, then rescuers go home relieved. If not, rescuers are on the scene earlier. In this case it would have meant the difference between a dry, quick rescue and a wet, cold, more dangerous one.

While hiking out with the stranded party, RMRG learned that they were college students who feared they could not afford the costs of a rescue. They said, "We didn't know that the rescuers were volunteers and that they don't charge to rescue people." Temperatures that night fell to near freezing. Luckily the underdressed climbers were still able to function and assist in their own rescue. (Source: Rocky Mountain Rescue Group.)

STRANDED – WEATHER, INEXPERIENCE
Boulder, First Flatiron

About 9:45 p.m. on June 28, the Boulder County Communications Center received a call from three climbers (two males, one female) stuck on the first pitch of Fandango (5.5) on the First Flatiron. Not long after that, an intense storm cell moved over the area, bringing hail, heavy rain, and widespread lightning. According to one of the climbers, the group took shelter under a huge flake to the right of the route, with lightning striking the cliff within 20 meters on all sides of the group.

Personnel from Rocky Mountain Rescue Group, Boulder Open Space and Mountain Parks, American Medical Response, and the Boulder County Sheriff's Office responded to their call for help and reached the climbers at about 11 p.m. By 1:15 a.m. all three had been evacuated off the rock without injury.

Analysis

This incident was documented by the group on a smartphone and posted online. In the video one of the male climbers remarks that there is a thunderstorm in the area and the group has decided to climb anyway. At the top of the first pitch, one of the climbers notes, "The rain has stopped, there are clouds rolling in, and it is getting dark. This is going to be an adventure." Darkness and the thunderstorm eventually overtake the group. The video shows one of the climbers calling 911 and asking the operator "are we safe?", and then asking if they "should be taking off metal objects." Fortunately the group stayed dry in the cave where they sought refuge, and even more fortunately none of the climbers was injured by a lightning strike or ground currents. Given the time of day and thunderstorms in the area, the group should not have started the climb. Shallow caves or chimneys are no place to be in a thunderstorm. (Sources: Boulder County Sheriff's Office and Aram Attarian.)

STRANDED – DARKNESS, INADEQUATE EQUIPMENT
Eldorado Canyon State Park

About 6 p.m. on January 26, Tim Holm (22), Davis Gray (22), and Josh Jordan (21) became stranded on the fifth pitch of the Yellow Spur (5.10a) on Redgarden Wall. Rescuers received a call for assistance from another climber in the area, who reported hearing a male yelling for help. The reporting party yelled back at the stranded climber and asked if he wanted a rescue. The stranded climber responded, "Yes." Twelve rescuers from the Rocky Mountain Fire Department, Rocky Mountain Rescue Group, Boulder Emergency Squad, and the Boulder County Sheriff's Office climbed to the top of the Redgarden Wall and contacted the stranded climbers at about 8 p.m. All were assisted to the ground with no injuries. (Source: Joe Rubino.)

Analysis

The climbers reported that as they neared the top of the Yellow Spur they had to wait for a slower group above them. It became dark and started raining, and they were not equipped with headlamps or flashlights. When climbing during winter months, climbers should anticipate shorter daylight hours, colder temperatures, and changing weather conditions. In preparation, climbers should carry extra clothing, a headlamp, food, and water. When attempting multi-pitch routes, it's prudent to research escape options and note rappel anchors en route in case you are unable to complete the ascent. (Source: Aram Attarian.)

FALL ON ROCK
Eldorado Canyon State Park

On March 17 at 11:15 a.m., Boulder County Sheriff's Office, Rocky Mountain Rescue, and Rocky Mountain Fire responded to Eldorado State Park on a report of a fallen climber. Rocky Mountain Fire and Rocky Mountain Rescue located the injured party, who was identified as Scott Clark (28). Scott was climbing with friends when he fell approximately 30 feet. He was evacuated and transported to Boulder Community Hospital with minor injuries. (Source: Boulder County Sheriff's Office.)

(*Editor's note: There are several similar incidents from this park each year. We do not put them all in the narrative section. A 30-foot fall is significant, but unless there is an explanation of how or why it happened, there are no takeaways.*)

FALL ON ROCK, BOULDERING
Eldorado Canyon State Park

On May 11 a man (32) was bouldering Germ Free Adolescence (V5+) when he intentionally let go rather than attempt to downclimb or continue up. He fell about 10 feet straight onto a crash pad. Despite a spotter assisting his landing, the fall badly broke the climber's right ankle, possibly due to a rock that was under the center of the crash pad. (Source: Steve Muehlhauser, Ranger, Eldorado Canyon State Park.)

Analysis

Multiple pads may be needed to protect a rocky landing under boulder problems. In addition, boulderers need to watch out for gaps in the padding, either between pads or where a foldable pad is hinged. (Source: Aram Attarian.)

STRANDED – DARKNESS, INADEQUATE EQUIPMENT
Eldorado Canyon State Park, Redgarden Wall

On August 15 at 1 a.m., Rocky Mountain Rescue Group, Rocky Mountain Fire, an American Medical Response ambulance, and the Boulder County Sheriff's Office responded to Redgarden Wall due to a report of a stranded climber. Kyle Willis (27) and Ryan Watts (24) had been climbing in the area and became separated after dark. Ryan was able to make it down, and then happened to run into Allison Sheets, a member of Rocky Mountain Rescue Group. She summoned other team members, and they were able to successfully guide Kyle down to the base. He was uninjured. (Source: Boulder County Sheriff's Office.)

Analysis

When climbing late in the day, climbers should carry a headlamp along with equipment and clothing to sustain them through the night if necessary. (Source: Aram Attarian.)

FALL ON ROCK, INADEQUATE PROTECTION – RAPPEL ERROR
Clear Creek Canyon

On April 6 a male climber (62) was killed after falling from the top of Levada (5.8+), an 80-foot rock climb at the far west end of the Canal Zone crag. According to witnesses, he was off belay and standing on top of the route, and was beginning to clean the anchor in order to rappel. He fell in a horizontal position without a rope, landing on his side and ending up face down. All of the quickdraws were still attached to the route. The anchor was still in place, equipped with locking carabiners and runners. The rope, locking carabiners, and figure-8 rappel device landed in a pile next to the cliff.

Analysis

Based on the limited amount of information presented, it is difficult to determine exactly what happened. However, this incident should reinforce a fundamental of rappelling or cleaning anchors for lowering: The climber must remain attached to the anchor until he or she is ready to rappel or be lowered. (Source: Mark Vermeal.)

FALL ON ROCK, CAM PULLED OUT
Staunton State Park

On September 29 a male fell while leading an unnamed route on Elk Creek Spires, on the north side of the park. His top piece of protection, a camming device, pulled out. He lost consciousness in the fall and suffered a fractured arm. Evacuation required the use of a helicopter. (Source: Mountainproject.com.)

Analysis

Cams pulling out under load—whether because of poor placement or poor rock—are frequently cited in our reports. Expert instruction is essential for proper use of cams. If there's any doubt about a piece's security, back it up if possible. (Source: Aram Attarian.)

FALL ON ROCK, CLIMBING ALONE AND UNROPED
Elk Mountains, Thunder Pyramid

On June 23, Steve Gladbach (52), a highly experienced mountaineer, was reported missing by two companions who had summited Thunder Pyramid (13,932 feet) with him. Gladbach was downclimbing and was ahead of his partners when they realized he had not arrived at a rendezvous point. Gladbach had told them that he was going to check out a waterfall that he planned to climb next winter.

The climbers searched for Gladbach for a couple of hours before activating their SPOT. A helicopter search was unsuccessful. A National Guard Black Hawk helicopter dropped eight members of Mountain Rescue Aspen (MRA) onto the mountain on June 24. The pilot then decided to search another area and spotted Gladbach's body. MRA members recovered the body, which was flown to Maroon Lake and then driven to Aspen Valley Hospital.

Analysis

Thunder Pyramid is regarded as one of Colorado's most dangerous mountains. It has been site of several deadly accidents over the years. Gladbach likely fell a couple of hundred feet on terrain notorious for its loose rock and exposure. (Source: Chad Abraham, *Aspen Daily News*.)

FALL ON ROCK, FAILURE TO FOLLOW ROUTE, LACK OF COMMUNICATION
Elk Mountains, Capitol Peak

On July 19 at 7 p.m., the Pitkin County Sheriff's Office received the report of an overdue climber on Capitol Peak (14,130 feet). Climbing partners stated that after reaching the summit via the northeast ridge (which requires crossing the exposed, Class 4 Knife Edge ridge), Ryan Palmer (35) attempted to climb down the north face rather than negotiate the northeast ridge a second time. He did this without discussion with his climbing partners. Palmer's partners continued to descend the route across the Knife Edge and could see Palmer as he worked his way down the north face. When he didn't arrive in camp, they decided to hike out and report him overdue.

On July 20, Mountain Rescue Aspen sent an airplane with spotters to look

for Palmer. They were unable to locate any signs of him, but determined which areas were most probable for the missing climber to be. Mountain Rescue Aspen sent foot teams into the field. Two teams took separate trails up to Capitol Lake, and then one team climbed to the base of the north face while the other interviewed climbers in the area. At 2:10 p.m., the team located a body matching the description of Palmer at the base of the north face.

[This page] The Knife Edge on Capitol Peak. The north face is on the right. *Josh Lewis*

Analysis

Capitol Peak is known for its exposure and loose rock—it is one of the most difficult of Colorado's fourteeners to climb. Taking the standard descent route, the Knife Edge, would have been the most prudent choice, as the route has relatively solid rock and the climbing party would have been familiar with some of the objective dangers. Authorities speculate that Palmer assumed he could find an easier descent route. (Source: Deputy Adam Crider, Pitkin County Sheriff's Office.)

FALL ON ROCK, FREE SOLO CLIMBING, OFF ROUTE
Montrose, Black Canyon of the Gunnison National Park

On July 10 the body of Andrew M. Barnes (27) was found at the base of the Painted Wall below Serpent Point. Based on evidence found at the scene, and also from talking to his friends and climbing partners, investigators believe he was attempting to free solo the Southern Arête (5.10 R). However, his body was located a few hundred feet up-river from the actual Southern Arête route. Investigators found a handwritten topo of the Southern Arête in his vehicle and have reason to believe he did not have another copy with him. They believe he got off route at some point and fell. No climbing gear other than his climbing shoes and a chalk bag were found.

Analysis

The Black Canyon is notorious for difficult routefinding as well as loose rock. This route faces south, making it quite hot in July. (Source: Matt Abraham, Black Canyon of the Gunnison National Park.)

ROCKFALL, POOR POSITION, INADEQUATE EQUIPMENT
San Juan Mountains, El Diente Peak

During the weekend of June 29-30, my son and I climbed the North Buttress Route (Class 3) on El Diente Peak (14,165 feet) and subsequently made the traverse to Mt. Wilson (14,252 feet). We had four experienced people in our party and were careful to stay out of the fall line of each other. To save time, we had two people climbing in lockstep near each other, so that if the lead climber triggered rockfall it would not have much momentum before hitting his partner.

The last third of the El Diente–Wilson traverse contained a lot of bad rock. We considered descending and walking below the last ridge, but there was a big snowfield with soft snow covering a sheet of ice. It didn't present a good option.

To address the situation, two members of our party climbed the 50-foot "staircase" that leads to a catwalk. We watched them disappear over the top and waited for them to be completely off the climb before following. We yelled a few times to confirm it was safe to follow, but could not hear their reply. We started up the staircase (Class 3). After approximately 10 feet my partner asked to lead the pitch since he was a better climber. I had stepped aside onto a small ledge to let him take the lead when one of the climbers above knocked loose a small pebble from the top of the ridge. The pebble hit a large rock, causing it tumble. In turn the rock hit a boulder, causing a few thousand pounds of rock to start falling down the staircase.

I was very fortunate to be protected on that side ledge. I received a small blow to the cheek but nothing severe. My helmet effectively blocked the small debris that rained down on me. With my body pressed against the cliff, I watched as dozens of rocks whizzed past me.

My partner was not as lucky. He was right in the middle of the staircase with no protection. Luckily, he managed to jump off a 10-foot cliff, take a couple of bounds, and get himself out of harm's way. At least 10 boulders big enough to crush us fell down the staircase. (Source: Edited from an anonymous report at 14ers.com.)

Analysis

Loose rock is an unavoidable hazard on some "classic" ridge traverses. To minimize the dangers, avoid climbing below others (wait until they have cleared the area), climb "nose to butt" so rockfall can't gain momentum between members of the party, test handholds with a rap of your palm against the rock, climb early in the morning, and always wear a helmet. This party did all of these things and yet was fortunate to escape without serious injury. (Source: Aram Attarian.)

KENTUCKY

FALL ON ROCK, ATTEMPTING TO CLIP BOLT
Muir Valley

On March 7 a male climber, about 20 years old, fell on lead while attempting to clip the first bolt and sustained a fractured ankle when he impacted the ground.

Analysis

Muir Valley provides loaner stick clips at no charge to its visitors. This climber declined to borrow one. Identical accidents happened in September and October. (Source: Rick Weber, Muir Valley.)

FALL ON ROCK, CARABINER BROKE – IMPROPERLY LOADED
Red River Gorge, The Flank Wall

On March 29 a climber on Mercy the Huff (5.12b) fell at the eighth bolt. This bolt is located at the lip of a little black "rooflet." After clipping the bolt, the climber made a long move to a crimp, attempted to make another move, and fell. The bolt-side carabiner on the draw "snapped" at the top radius in the fall, resulting in a longer and scarier ride than expected. The climber was not injured. (Source: Edited from a report at Redriverclimbing.com.)

Analysis

Best guess is that the climber either kicked or snagged the draw while making the next long move, causing the carabiner to shift on the bolt hanger. During the fall, the carabiner broke because it was not meant to be loaded on other than its main axis. Carabiners have been known to break in such fashion due to the carabiner being snagged, rotated, or cross-loaded on the bolt hanger.

What can be learned from this, and how this could have been prevented?

• Check the bolt placement to make sure that when a carabiner is clipped into the hanger the spine on the 'biner is not exposed to any levering action which might cause it to break during a fall. If so, try a different carabiner or quickdraw that might alleviate the problem. Using a more flexible "trad" draw might prevent the draw and carabiner from shifting on the bolt hanger.

• Double-check your draws to make sure they are hanging properly and not snagged or twisted.

• Avoid kicking or shifting your draws as you climb past them.

• Note that you really aren't out of the "danger zone" when sport climbing until you are fairly high on the route.

• Try to avoid falling when you have only one draw clipped. (Sources: Redriverclimbing.com and Aram Attarian.)

FALLING ROCK
Red River Gorge, Global Village

On May 13, I (Matt Queen, 32) was gearing up at the base of Father and Son (5.7) when a member of my party, climbing above me, dislodged a block weighing approximately 10 pounds while traversing between the anchors of Father and Son and the adjacent route Kentucky Pinstripe. Both routes start on a very large ledge. I had my back turned to the cliff when I was struck on the top of my helmeted head and knocked unconscious. Members of my party noted that the climber above yelled, "Rock!" but I don't remember hearing the warning. After the impact, another member in my party grabbed me and kept me from falling off the ledge. I regained consciousness after about one minute. After I had gathered myself and was checked for further injuries, I was evacuated by the three members of my group.

Analysis

• My helmet probably saved my life. Always wear a helmet while climbing, especially where rockfall is possible.

• Be aware of what's happening around you. If I had paying more attention to the others climbing, I might have been able to avoid the falling rock.

• Assess potential hazards while climbing, Although both routes were well traveled, the traverse between the two anchors was not, therefore greatly increasing the possibility of encountering loose rock.

• Assess the hazards of the surrounding environment at the base of the cliff. Because the ledge at the base was so large, the thought of being knocked off it had not occurred to anyone.

• Take a Wilderness First Responder or Wilderness First Aid course to be prepared when situations such as this arise. (Source: Matt Queen.)

FALL ON ROCK, INEXPERIENCD BELAYER, IMPROPER USE OF A GRIGRI, NO HELMET
Muir Valley, The Boneyard

On April 20, a male lead climber (23) was put on belay by his partner (male, 19) with a brand-new Grigri. The belayer had never used a Grigri before. As the climber moved up the belayer squeezed the Grigri shut with his left hand while pulling out rope for the leader with his right. The leader fell, continued unarrested 30 feet, and landed on a boulder. The belayer, in a desperate attempt to arrest the fall, gripped the rope flying out of the Grigri, damaging the skin on the palm of his hand.

Two Muir Valley Rescue volunteers were nearby and called out the rescue group immediately after the fall. Additional rescuers, including an emergency room nurse who happened to be on site, responded to the call. Ten minutes into the operation, rescuers called for a helicopter and the Wolfe County SAR Team to assist if needed. The carry out from the cliff went very smoothly. The climber was transported to the waiting helicopter and flown to a level-one trauma center in Lexington. He suffered lacerations and a concussion. He wasn't wearing a helmet. (Source: Rick Weber, Muir Valley.)

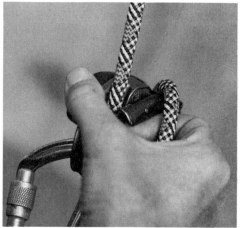

[This page] The best hand position for feeding rope quickly through a Grigri. With this method the brake hand never leaves the rope. *Erik Rieger*

Analysis

The Grigri is designed as an assisted-braking device, and both trained and untrained belayers often get a false sense of security while using it. Overall, the Grigri is a safe and effective device in the hands of an experienced user. It's important to note that the manufacturer has never marketed the Grigri as a "hands-free" belay device. Petzl recommends that it is for expert use only, and notes that, "as with all climbing and mountaineering activities, it is essential to master the techniques and understand the limitations on using this product in these activities. Practice the techniques...in a managed environment before using them in a real situation." (Source: Aram Attarian.)

(Editor's note: Excellent instructional information on using a Grigri properly, including a video tutorial, can be found at Petzl.com/en/outdoor/belay-devices/grigri.)

FALL ON ROCK, OVERCONFIDENCE, NUT PULLED OUT
Red River Gorge, Pistol Ridge

On September 28 a male climber named Roro fell while climbing Way of the Peaceful Warrior (5.10a). He fell off the bouldery first section of the route, and his first placement (a No. 8 nut) behind a thin flake pulled. This section of the route is very tricky to protect and run-out.

Analysis

Roro noted, "As I geared up for the climb, I was completely confident in my ability to add this route to my tick list. As I bouldered past the chossy initial section and placed my first piece in the crack, I wished for a rack with doubles since I saved a potential good first piece for later on the route. That was my mistake. I should have placed the most bomber piece as soon as I had the opportunity and not be concerned about what was higher on the route. However, having made quick work of a 10b a couple of days earlier, and this being a 10a, I believed that I would fare well on the route.

"I fell 25 feet and pulled the piece with me, and I suffered a compression fracture. I'm extremely lucky to be around and able to write this, all thanks to a helmet protecting my head." (Source: Edited from a post on Rockmerica. wordpress.com.)

RAPPEL ERROR – NO KNOTS ON ENDS OF ROPE, LACK OF COMMUNICATION
Red River Gorge, Muir Valley

Late in the afternoon on October 6, a male climber (22), after cleaning the anchors on Rat Stew (5.10a), a 75-foot climb, fell approximately 60 feet after rappelling off the end of one of his rope strands. He suffered internal injuries, including a lacerated lung, broken ribs, two broken vertebrae, a head contusion, and a concussion.

Analysis

According to reports, he did not check to be sure both ends of his rope were on the ground, nor did his belayer warn him the ropes were grossly uneven. He also did not tie blocking knots on the rope ends. (Source: Rick Weber, Muir Valley.)

FALL ON ROCK, FAILURE TO CLIP BOLT
Red River Gorge, Muir Valley

On October 6 a male climber (35) took a long lead fall while reaching high for a bolt. His fall caused him to impact a tree. He suffered broken ribs, a punctured/collapsed lung, and broken scapula, requiring surgical repair. (Source: Rick Weber, Muir Valley.)

Analysis

Overreaching forces one's center of gravity into the rock and may cause one's feet to lose their grip. Sometimes it's best to climb one or two moves higher to a better stance before clipping. Also consider the use of a stiff "cheater draw" for reaching distant bolts. Or use a stick clip. (Source: Aram Attarian.)

MAINE

FALL ON ROCK – PROTECTION PULLED OUT, NO HELMET
Acadia National Park, The Precipice, Old Town

On April 28, Will Raymond (age 21) was leading Old Town, a popular 5.7 corner climb. Nearing the top of the first corner, which is typically climbed as a lieback, he slipped and fell. The camming unit that he had placed for protection failed, and he fell to the ground. He was not wearing a helmet and suffered head and spine injuries. He was evacuated to the local hospital by NPS rangers and Mount Desert Island SAR, and then taken by Lifeflight to a trauma center where he was treated and recovered very well.

Analysis

This climb, while protectable with a wide variety of gear, requires careful attention to the direction of placements, especially low on the climb where the pull of the rope could cause upward forces to occur. Using slings to minimize movement of gear placements and placing gear close together at the start of a pitch are almost always good ideas. (Source: Jon Tierney, IFMGA Mountain Guide.)

FALL ON ROCK – LOWERING ERROR
Acadia National Park, The Precipice, Old Town

On July 17, Andrea Campanella (47), a guide with a local climbing company, was guiding two older teenagers on the South Wall of Champlain Mountain when he fell to the ground due to a lowering error. The exact sequence of events is not clear, due to memory deficits, and has been reconstructed from conversations with the clients and a nearby guide.

At roughly 1 p.m., after climbing several routes in the morning, Andrea led Old Town (5.7) to a two-bolt anchor with stainless-steel rings. It is believed that he then passed the rope through the anchor rings, set a directional piece, and was lowered down Connecticut Cracks (5.11), intending to demonstrate that climb for the stronger climber. On the ground, he likely pulled the rope taut through the anchor to the belayer and then clipped into the rope, roughly in the middle, via a figure-8 on a bight and two carabiners (one locking). He then had the second client tie in at the end that he had just untied from. He demonstrated the moves on Connecticut Cracks and clipped the trailing rope into the directional. Upon reaching the anchor, he secured himself and belayed the stronger climber up CC, and then lowered the climber to the ground, at which point the climber likely untied. Andrea then detached himself from the anchor with the intent of being lowered, planning to clean pieces from Old Town and leave CC set up. Intending to be lowered via the rope on the Old Town side of the system (which would have had enough rope), he was actually lowered with the rope on the CC side, which did not have enough rope for him to reach the ground. He was lowered several feet and had removed several pieces from Old Town before the end of the rope slipped through the belayer's device and Andrea fell approximately 30 feet to the ground.

Local guide Dick Chasse, guiding on an adjacent route, reached Andrea in less than five minutes. He provided emergency care and called for NPS evacuation. Andreas was evacuated with personnel from the NPS and Mount Desert Island SAR, and was airlifted to Eastern Maine Medical Center. He suffered significant injuries to his head and chest. Fortunately, he has made a nearly full recovery.

Analysis

The above is a "best guess" as to how the accident occurred. There are a number of contributing factors as well, certainly the most important being that the end of the belay side of the rope was no longer secured at the time of lowering. Other factors may include miscommunication between the guide and the belayer, and an attempt to set up an overly complicated rope system.

Originally from Italy, Andrea has a 25-year climbing history that spans Europe, the U.S., and South America on a variety of rock, ice, and mountaineering routes. He holds a Ph.D. in biology and worked previously as a wildlife biologist. He recently completed the AMGA Rock Instructor course and had participated in several days of additional guide training. (Source: Jon Tierney, IFMGA Mountain Guide.)

(Editor's note: Jon Tierney also reported briefly that in June there was an accident in which a climber fell while soloing a tower at Monument Cove, resulting in significant injuries to the head, extremities, and spine. Late in the summer a guide fell from Central Slabs due to an improperly rigged rappel transition, resulting in significant leg extremity and minor spine injuries. In the fall a Camden climber fell after ascending a sport route because the rappel/lower was improperly set up.)

MINNESOTA

FALL ON ROCK – ROPE SEVERED ON SHARP EDGE, INADEQUATE PROTECTION
Sandstone

A party of approximately 15 volunteers was cleaning routes for the ice climbing season. Volunteers' levels of experience ranged from great to little. The victim volunteered to go on rappel to clean the face of a new route and was handed an 11mm static rope. Having no other gear with her and assuming the risk would be small, she tied the rope to a tree, double-checked her systems, and rappelled down to clean the route. After one route was successfully cleaned, she climbed back up and tied off in a new spot to continue cleaning.

For efficiency, she was clearing an area on the wall with a width of

[This page] Example of rope protection for an anchor or top-rope. *Spiroll Rope Protectors*

approximately 30 feet, moving from side to side. About two feet below the top of the cliff, however, the rope was rubbing on a sharp edge of sandstone that was just barely visible to people who inspected the area after the accident. That edge ended up severing the rope, and she fell about 30 feet to the ground. A lucky landing left her only with two stable fractures, one in her vertebrae and one in her pelvis.

Analysis

This accident might have been prevented by the use of edge protectors, a better understanding of the type of rock and its susceptibility to erosion and sharpness, an anchor system that extended over the sharp edge, a more thorough inspection for sharp or rough edges, and less horizontal movement while on rappel. (Source: Kathleen Loughran, 22.)

MONTANA

FALL ON ROCK, INADEQUATE PROTECTION
Hyalite Canyon, Practice Rock

On September 2, John "Amos" Ridenour (35), a Gallatin County sheriff's deputy, died after falling while rock climbing in Hyalite Canyon, 10 miles south of Bozeman. He had gone to Practice Rock with his son and neighbor early on Labor Day morning to teach the boy how to climb, said Sheriff Brian Gootkin.

Ridenour climbed the route to manage the rope work from above, said Gootkin. At 8:20 a.m., while atop the rock, Ridenour fell about 35 to 40 feet. (Source: Adapted from an article by Ason Bacaj in the *Bozeman Daily Chronicle*.)

FALL ON ROCK, INADEQUATE PROTECTION
Hyalite Canyon, Practice Rock

On September 21 a climber named Michael Parker fell 30 to 40 feet from Practice Rock. Officials said Parker had failed to secure his anchor. It took more than 35 rescuers about an hour and a half to get him off the side of the mountain, due to rough terrain. Parker had suffered a broken ankle, broken lumbar vertebrae, and a head injury. He was transported to Bozeman Deaconess Hospital and then airlifted to St. Vincent's Hospital in Billings. (Source: KBZK News.)

(*Editor's note: It seems likely that both Mr. Ridenour and Mr. Parker were in the process of setting up anchor systems in order to establish top-rope belays. The lesson from these two incidents is that we need to always secure ourselves in an exposed situation before setting up the belay system.*)

NEVADA

STRANDED, FAILED TO FOLLOW ROUTE – INADEQUATE FOOD/WATER/ CLOTHING/EQUIPMENT
Red Rock, Pine Creek Canyon, Cat in the Hat

My climbing partner, Marty Goss (50) and I, Paul Spence (52), met at Red Rock for a week of climbing. On March 14 we had planned to climb Cat in the Hat, a six-pitch 5.6 trad route in Pine Creek Canyon. We were the only ones on the route and could see another set of climbers on the opposite wall across the canyon. By the time we were on the fifth pitch, a pair of faster climbers had caught up with us. They were smooth and very efficient at building anchors.

Sometime late in the climb, we could hear someone calling for assistance. We thought was coming from the climbers across the canyon, but we couldn't see them. During our second rappel from the top, we realized the calls for assistance were actually coming from climbers who were stranded below us. As best we could decipher, their rope didn't reach the ground during their last rappel. When we reached our fourth rappel station, we decided we would rappel down to assist the stranded pair.

While the climbers above us angled to the left to access the normal descent route, Marty and I rappelled down the fall line to reach the stranded climbers. Before rappelling, we confirmed with the stranded climbers that we could reach the ground from their location with two ropes (ours and theirs combined). Marty rappelled first. As soon as he could, Marty confirmed that our rope would indeed reach the stranded couple before committing to the rappel any farther.

Upon reaching the young college couple, he found them standing on an 18-inch ledge. He learned they were on spring break with friends from University of

Utah. The gal was anchored into a small tree, and the guy wasn't anchored into anything. He was just standing on the ledge and not tied in. Neither had helmets. Marty told the guy to immediately tie into the tree. It was getting toward the end of the day, and the sun was setting beyond the canyon walls. The gal, who was wearing short shorts and a halter top, was getting cold. As it turned out, they had started climbing Cat in the Hat and had accidentally gotten off route. After getting into some much more difficult climbing, they decided to do some intense downclimbing and rap off the route. As they were not on a standard descent route, they became stranded.

Analysis

Their equipment was on the lean side, and neither of them had a jacket. They had learned to climb in the gym and eventually progressed to trad climbing in Big Cottonwood Canyon, east of Salt Lake City. They owned a guidebook but had chosen to leave it at camp, thinking they wouldn't need it. Neither of them used auto-block back-ups on their rappels, so I rapped first to provide a fireman's belay from the ground. The landing was in a thicket of what seemed like holly bushes, so we gave the young lady one of our jackets so she wouldn't get too scratched up getting out of there. We all eventually made it back to our packs at the base of the climb.

Granted, this turned out to be a mild incident, but I believe today's climber can learn much from it. Outside of not wanting to carry the weight, I can't see why you wouldn't bring your guidebook to a place and route you've never done before. What college student doesn't have a cell phone and not carry it everywhere? Next time, take a picture of the route page in the guidebook.

The couple started the climb late in the day and had no extra layers or water with them. Their sparse rack might have limited their rappelling options as well.

After climbing for 35 years it's safe to say that I'm an old-school climber. Although it is purely opinion on my part, it seems that many of today's generation of climbers become great technical climbers while skipping many of the basics. Many come from the gym environment. Then they get their harnesses, shoes, belay devices, and rope and head out into the world of unforgiving gravity. If they drop a belay device from on high, they're stuck because no one ever taught them to improvise a body belay. It seems that many don't give a thought of carrying an extra 'biner or even a prusik cord to help them out in a jam. And as we know, all of us eventually get into a jam. Let's help each other out, folks, because it seems like we're raising a generation of 5.12 climbers with 5.5 knowledge of how to deal with the predicaments we find ourselves in while climbing. (Source: Edited from a report by Paul Spence.)

(*Editor's note: We can suggest one benefit of not always carrying a guidebook: Every climb you do will feel like a first ascent. Learning how to figure out the route—and being able to downclimb when you have reached a point beyond your level—builds skill and confidence. Just be sure you have the gear and knowledge to get out of whatever predicaments climbing "blind" will get you into.*)

NEW HAMPSHIRE

AVALANCHE – POOR POSITION, INADEQUATE EQUIPMENT
Mt. Washington, Huntington Ravine, Central Gully

On January 17 a party of 12 was ascending Central Gully in Huntington Ravine in four teams when one rope team triggered a soft slab avalanche. The avalanche swept over the three other rope teams, carrying one to the bottom of the gully. This team was not buried, but sustained injuries. The remaining three teams were able to rappel the route.

This was a fund-raising climb organized to raise awareness and support for Iraq war veterans. The climbers had been training for the climb in the days before the event, including ice climbing in Crawford Notch. The organized group included persons with a variety of experience and skills, from novice to experienced mountaineers. In addition, a film crew was present.

The group arrived at the Harvard Mountaineering Club cabin on Wednesday afternoon and spent the night in the cabin. Thursday morning, after receiving the weather forecast from the Mt. Washington Observatory, they decided to climb Central Gully. Before departing, a USFS snow ranger arrived and discussed weather and avalanche conditions with the group. Despite warnings of worsening avalanche danger, the group decided to stick with their plan. They departed from the cabin at 8:30 a.m.

Four hours after leaving the cabin, they arrived at the start of the climb. The group split into rope teams of three people each. They ascended to the ice bulge in the gully, and one by one climbed the bulge on belay. Above the ice bulge, the teams began simul-climbing. They reported that they skirted the newly deposited snow and tried to stay on the older crust. Prior to the avalanche, the lead team allowed the second team to pass so they could get set up for filming. At the time of the avalanche, one team was nearing the top of the gully and another was slightly below them and positioned in the center of the gully. The other two teams were lower, hugging the rock wall on climbers' left. During the time the teams were in avalanche terrain, snow continued to load many areas, including the

[This page] Central Gully. All four rope teams were in the upper half when the avalanche was triggered. *Mount Washington Avalanche Center*

top of Central Gully. (Source: Adapted from a report at Mountwashington-avalanchecenter.org.)

Analysis

At this year's annual Wilderness Risk Management Conference, Thom Pollard of Eyes Open Productions, who was filming this event, and Dr. Will White, director of Summit Achievements, presented a workshop called "Central Gully Avalanche, A Case Study: How Good Intentions Slide You Straight to Hell." They raised two important questions about the causes of the incident: Are good intentions dangerous? Do fund-raisers have an effect on decision-making? They also listed four heuristic traps: familiarity (among team members), social proof (the cause for which they were climbing), commitment (to the goal), and scarcity (having to do with the separation of the roped teams). A comprehensive analysis of this incident by USFS rangers is available at Mountwashingtonavalanchecenter.org/search-rescue/. Look in the 2012–2013 section under Incidents & Accidents.

AVALANCHE – CLIMBING ALONE AND UNROPED
Mt. Washington, Huntington Ravine, Pinnacle Gully

On March 1, James "Jimmy" Watts died as a result of injuries sustained in an avalanche in Pinnacle Gully. Jimmy left the Harvard Mountaineering Club cabin near the base of Huntington Ravine, intending to climb multiple gullies. Based on earlier conversations and by tracking his footprints in new snow, it's believe he climbed the ice pitches in Odell Gully. He then descended a snow ramp into the bottom of South Gully before heading up into Pinnacle. Approximately two-thirds of the way up the route, on what would be the second pitch for a roped party, Jimmy triggered a slab avalanche that carried him downslope. He was found by a climber halfway down the Fan (the talus slope in the lower portion of the ravine) at approximately 3 p.m. The climber, who is a physician, called 911 to report the accident. He reported that Jimmy had no vital signs. USFS snow rangers responded to the scene from Hermit Lake. They located Jimmy, confirmed his status, and prepared him for transport to Pinkham Notch.

The avalanche released in the upper portion of the second pitch of the ice climb, just below a narrowing formed by exposed rock in the gully. The crown line was about 20 to 30 feet uphill from where we believe the climber was when the avalanche released. The crown was two feet deep, 20 feet wide, and slid on a bed surface of water ice. Avalanche danger on the day of the incident was rated "moderate."

Analysis

Jimmy Watts was a strong mountaineer with seven years of climbing experience, and was president of the Harvard Mountaineering Club from 2009 to 2010. He had spent dozens of winter days on Mt. Washington over the years. He had climbed every gully in Huntington Ravine, including Pinnacle, multiple times. All of the gullies were well within his technical abilities. Jimmy had read about and studied the dynamics of avalanches, and gained decision-making experience from years of mountaineering and backcountry snowboarding. However, he had never taken a formal avalanche safety course.

At the time of the accident he had been climbing on the mountain and staying at the Harvard Cabin at the base of Huntington Ravine for several days. He was well aware of the recent snow cycle and weather conditions on the mountain. A few days before the accident he climbed Pinnacle and Damnation gullies with a partner. On the day of the accident he read the posted avalanche report and discussed his plans with the Harvard Cabin caretaker and the Mt. Washington snow rangers.

Jimmy knew he might encounter unfavorable conditions, and even though he was climbing solo he carried a pack containing all the equipment he might need for retreat: a 60-meter rope, harness, and anchor-building materials for ice and rock. Of course, this equipment could do nothing in the event of a sudden hazard such as an unexpected avalanche.

The avalanche that killed Jimmy was not large. He was not buried and did not suffocate, but instead died from internal injuries caused by his fall. Had the avalanche occurred in lower-consequence terrain, he likely would have been unhurt. However, once above the first-pitch ice bulge in Pinnacle, any fall would have been severe.

The Jimmy we knew liked to go for it, and it was one of his many admirable qualities. He was no doubt trying to balance this enthusiasm against rational risk calculations and his love of life. In the end, it all added up to a decision to go. It's a good opportunity to reflect on our own decision-making processes and what goes into them. (Source: Edited from a report submitted by Will Skinner and various members of the Harvard Mountaineering Club.)

FALL ON ICE, CLIMBING ALONE AND UNROPED
Crawford Notch, Frankenstein Cliffs

Mark, Pete, and I (Jesse Morenz) headed up to the Whites early Saturday morning, March 16, to train for our upcoming Liberty Ridge climb. We arrived at the Frankenstein parking lot at 12:30 p.m. and planned on getting in two climbs before our larger alpine climb the next day. We decided to climb the first two pitches of Standard and then finish with the Penguin. At the base of the route we encountered an older climber (mid-60s). He was by himself and seemed a bit off. Not thinking much of it, we headed up the first pitch of Standard. Pete led up to the cave on the right side and set up a belay, bringing Mark and I up. At the cave we arranged ourselves and then Mark headed up the second pitch. After Mark began, we heard a sound that is hard to describe, but all of us knew what it was: the sound of a falling climber. I looked down to see the older climber cartwheeling down the lower portion of the route, all the way to the railroad tracks below. At first I thought he had slipped at the base of the route and tumbled down. I quickly realized that he was moving too fast—he had fallen off the first pitch of Standard Center while soloing.

Other than curl into a fetal position, he did not move after impact; this was a very serious injury or a fatality. At the tracks, four or so climbers reached him nearly instantly. They dispatched two runners to call 911 and get the litter from the emergency cache at the parking area. As this was happening, I called down to see if they needed help. They told me that they would need us to help carry him out. Being mindful of our own safety, Mark carefully downclimbed back to the cave and all three of us rapped down, leaving the rope in place.

The first climbers on the scene had bandaged the victim's head wound and taken his pulse, led by an IMCS guide. He was not unconscious, but was barely speaking. He was complaining about his hip and saying he could not breathe. He was gurgling when he took a breath. One of the runners returned with the litter and the group lifted him onto it, securing him with climbing rope and webbing. Then the group lifted the litter and carried the victim out. Climbers, many still in full gear, took turns keeping his airway clear. He complained from time to time that he could not breathe, but as time passed these complaints decreased.

More and more climbers joined the rescue party as we walked down the tracks; over 15 climbers were assisting with the rescue by the time we got to the trestle. I expected to see snow machines on the other side of the trestle, but there were none. We carried him out the entire way. Very close to the parking area, a few EMTs met us. At the parking area we transferred the man onto a gurney and the EMTs put him in the ambulance. We were informed that they planned to take him to an area where a medical helicopter could land and transport him to Dartmouth's hospital.

Analysis

My thoughts on the matter are, first and foremost, solo ice climbing is dangerous. This was the second major incident in a few weeks in the Whites involving a solo ice climber. The second is that one should not expect a major rescue if injured. This accident happened under the best possible conditions for a rescue. It was on a frequently climbed route, and there were many people around. Even so, it took 80 minutes to get the victim to the ambulance. If an injury occurred in a more remote area of the White Mountains, like Mt. Willey, it could be many hours before anyone responded. One must remember these rescue personnel are volunteers from a small town—in this case Bartlett. They did everything right, but they do not have the staff or resources to get paramedics to an injured climber in 15 minutes (or even an hour). What one can rely on is help from the tribe—every climber who saw the incident helped. But they can only help if they are around. (Source: Jesse Morenz.)

FALL ON ROCK, RAPPEL ERROR – UNEVEN AND UNKNOTTED ROPES
Cathedral Ledge, Child's Play

My climbing partner and I were involved in a rescue on July 23 when a climber in his early 20s fell while descending Child's Play (5.5) at Cathedral Ledge. We had just come down from Recluse at the North End and were packing up around 2:30 p.m. A party had finished Child's Play, the line directly to the right of Recluse. They were descending via rappel from a tree on the North End belay ledge. The first climber had thrown the ropes such that one end was about 25 feet above the ground. He had rappelled just past the bulging ledge about midway up Child's Play when the short end of the rope ran through his device. He fell to the ground, landing on his back. I inspected the rappel device. He had extended it and backed it up with a prusik, but the backup failed when one end, unknotted, slipped through.

He suffered serious lower back injuries, along with leg, arm, neck, and other injuries. He remained conscious the entire time, though in a lot of pain. Within 15 to 20 minutes of the fall, emergency services arrived, followed by SAR. He was stabilized, placed on a backboard, and carried out on a litter via the trail. He was in the ambulance by 3:30 p.m.

Analysis

It sucks that it takes an accident to reinforce the shit you already know you should do: Always tie knots in the ends of the rappel rope. I had rappelled to the ground just minutes before the accident, and I did not tie knots for the same reasons these climbers cited: "It's a short route, I've done the rap before, and I know the rope is long enough." Fortunately, I checked that I had my middle mark at the rings. These guys, for whatever reason, did not. One of the climber's friends had mentioned that they recently had a conversation about tying knots, and that the victim was normally a very safe climber. (Source: Anonymous.)

FALL ON ROCK, PROTECTION PULLED OUT – NO HELMET, EXCEEDING ABILITIES
Cathedral Ledge, Barber Wall, Nutcracker

On August 10 a climber in his mid to late 20s was leading Nutcracker (5.10a) on the Barber Wall. He fell and at least one of his pieces pulled, causing him to flip backward. He hit his head before falling to the ground. He was not wearing a helmet.

The Mountain Rescue Service mobilized, and after more than two hours of effort got him to the top, a little before dark. This required a litter carry along the traverse ledge, followed by a carry up the gully. At the top a waiting ambulance transported him to the local hospital.

Analysis

While often rated 5.9, this route is really 5.10a! It is a sustained crack climb requiring a variety of thin to moderate protection pieces. With modern cams it is possible to place good protection almost anywhere along the route. The climber's fall could have been mitigated if he had more experience placing gear. (Source: Al Hospers, Mountain Rescue Service.)

FALL ON ROCK, FALLING ROCK – FAILURE TO TEST HOLDS, INADEQUATE BELAY
Humphrey's Ledge, Tree Keys

According to two reports, someone fell after the second bolt on Tree Keys at the

Geriatric Walls on September 14. The belayer (age unknown) received significant rope burns on her hands.

As reported, the belayer lost control of the rope as the leader was falling when she tripped while trying to dodge rockfall. However, she then grabbed the rope above the belay device in order to slow the fall. She tried to get under the leader to cushion his fall with her body and keep him off the ground. The leader hit the ground, but was probably saved significant injury due to her efforts.

Analysis

I was involved in developing this area and helped put up these routes. This particular climb has reasonable protection and bolts up to about 30 feet. Then there is a 15-foot section of fourth-class scrambling, going through a chimney to a ledge, and up to the next bolt on a nose. The day following the incident, local guide George Hurley and I did this climb to try to determine what happened.

Just below the bolt on the nose was a place where a rock obviously had been pulled off the ledge. George spotted a fresh rock the size of a baseball on the ground near the belay stance. There are no gear placements up through the chimney scramble leading to this point. Our assessment is that a fall from below the bolt, prior to clipping this protection, would result in almost certain ground-fall—not to mention the leader would bounce off the slab at the start!

I had climbed that route a week before and had not noticed any loose rocks. That said, I don't pull outward on any rocks in a place like that, and I always test handholds before putting my full weight on them.

There was a tree right at the natural stance at the base of the climb with a comfortable place to stand behind and beside it. Had the belayer been there, she easily could have ducked behind the tree to avoid the rock and never let go of the rope. (Source: Al Hospers, Mountain Rescue Service.)

FALL ON ROCK, CARABINER "UNCLIPPED" FROM BOLT
Rumney, Bonehead Roof

Bonehead Roof is a 5.10d climb with a classic "Rumney Runout": five bolts protect the route. The first bolt is about 20 feet off of the ground. The initial two-thirds of the climb are approximately 5.8, containing three bolts. A slope of about 20 or 30 degrees (not totally flat, but not very steep) for maybe 20 feet leads to the final leg of the climb, which is vertical, ending with an overhang that requires a mantel to finish (the crux).

On October 5, Eric (26) led this climb and only had difficulty with the crux. He tried and fell at least three times before finishing by an alternate route (the end of a different climb). After he finished I decided to try leading the climb. I had no trouble reaching the bottom of the overhang, where I clipped the fourth bolt before continuing up to clip the final bolt. I then went back and cleaned the fourth bolt to reduce rope drag.

I was able to mantel up over the overhang, but was unable to find a grip to clip into the chains. This caused me to fall backward, and I was caught by the rope clipped to the fifth bolt. I attempted the crux four times and was caught each time. I thought I would give the mantel one last try before completing the climb by another route. When I reached the top, I was again unable to maintain my balance and I fell backward, but this time, as I passed the fifth bolt, I watched my carabiner come unclipped from it. (No, I was not back-clipped, as that would have made my rope come unclipped from the quickdraw, not the quickdraw from the bolt.)

Because of the long run-out between bolts and my back-cleaning, the next piece was the quickdraw on the third bolt, only two-thirds of the way up the climb. I fell roughly 60 feet before the rope caught me about 15 or 20 feet from the ground.

I fell in a backward/horizontal position with my left hand in front of my face. Just before the rope stopped me, my left hand smacked the wall. This shattered my hand. I broke nine bones in total: my pinkie just above the knuckle, the knuckles on my ring and

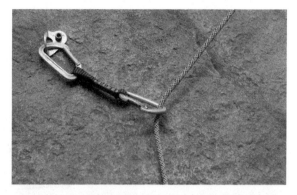

[This page] The lower carabiner on this quickdraw is oriented correctly, gate facing away from the direction of travel. But the upper 'biner should be oriented the same way on the draw. If the lead rope tugs the draw out of position, it can lever the gate against the bolt hanger, possibly unclipping. *Erik Rieger*

middle finger, a chip on my index finger near the base of the metacarpal, all of the metacarpals where they attach to the wrist, and a chip on my hamate. I also had a two-foot-long rope burn on my ribs and a healthy scrape on my left ankle. Overall, I am lucky I only broke my hand. I will say that that, although I did not hit my head, I was glad I was wearing my helmet.

Analysis

Carabiners can come unclipped from bolt hangers, rare though this may be. I believe in my instance the rope somehow pushed up and twisted the draw, and unclipped the carabiner. To make this climb safer I could have clipped a locking carabiner to the bolt or finished the climb by the other route and worked the crux on top-rope (probably the safest way). (Source: Walter Scott, 23.)

(Editor's note: There are several things you can do to minimize the chances of carabiners levering against bolt hangers and unclipping. The top (bolt-end) carabiner

should be "loose" in the dogbone or sling, never held tight by a rubber keeper. Quickdraws should be assembled with both carabiner gates oriented in the same direction, and draws should be clipped so the gates are oriented away from the direction of travel. Despite these precautions, a quickdraw may come unclipped from a bolt hanger. For that reason, it's never wise to skip bolts or other protection. If rope drag is an issue, use longer quickdraws or shoulder-length slings to reduce the drag.

Another comment from Joe Forrester, one of our editors: "Smart leaders, whether on sport or trad lines, always carry one or two draws or slings with locking carabiners for exactly this scenario. It can be challenging to predict fall lines when going over roofs, and having lockers on the bolts helps prevent odd cross-loading or unclipping incidents.")

NEW MEXICO

FALL ON ROCK, FALLING ROCK
Sandia Mountains

In the early afternoon of March 29, parties called 911 and reported "cries for help near the Upper La Luz Trail in Upper La Cueva Canyon." Bernalillo County Sheriff officers located Carlos Cox (35) by helicopter at the northeastern base of the Tridents, near the top of the upper, snow-covered couloir. There was no report of movement and large amounts of blood were seen from the air. Albuquerque Mountain Rescue and other SAR personnel were paged out at 2:30 p.m. Firefighters, already in the field, reached the subject and reported him dead.

Transfer of care of the subject was passed from the fire department to SAR personnel to perform a technical, low-angle snow and talus evacuation down to the La Luz Trail for a continued trail carry-out to the Sandia Crest.

Analysis

Carlos was an avid mountaineer and beloved member of Albuquerque Mountain Rescue. His fervor for becoming a great rescuer led him to evaluate likely rescue locations, including the week prior, when he was evaluating high-probability routes along Second Tower Ridge, over the Tridents, and on to the La Luz Trail. His return to the area on this day was a continuation of that project, according to family. On the morning of the 29th, Carlos notified family of his plan for the day and was equipped appropriately and prepared to handle a possible egress during his travels up his planned route. Carlos notified his family that he planned to travel alone. The atmospheric conditions in the Sandias that day were clear, warm, and dry.

This area of the Sandias is composed of highly fractured Precambrian granite, formed approximately 1.4 billion years ago. Over the past 10 years drastic drought conditions have killed many of the large trees and altered the delicate cliff microenvironment, leading to an accelerated erosive pattern. Larger freeze-thaw cycles are now active, where root systems and grasses once held topsoil in place, leading to increased lubrication and dislodgement of large rock features. This has been noted on trade routes where good rock protection was easily placed and now gear placements are dubious. Local climbing development has been geared toward face climbing and increased bolt placement rather than relying on traditional, removable protection.

Although the exact cause of Carlos' fall will never be known, it is highly likely that he passed across an unstable area that dislodged underneath him by surprise. This type of event in the Sandias has been repeated many times. It is very rare to have a climbing fatality while climbing an established route in the Sandias, however the approaches and descents are more dangerous, especially when unroped or on fourth-class terrain. (Source: Albuquerque Mountain Rescue, J. Marc Beverly, UIAGM Guide/Senior Rescue Leader, and Erin Weber, Technical Rescue Specialist.)

NEW YORK

RAPPEL ERROR – INADEQUATE PROTECTION, CLIMBING ALONE, INEXPERIENCED
Albany, Thatcher Park

On September 18, Ronald Czajkowski (44) fell 120 feet to his death at Thatcher Park, according to police. "He had a harness and rope with him. It appears it was human error as far as attaching it to the anchor point on top of the cliff," said Captain John Layton from the Albany County Sheriff's Department.

Layton said Czajkowski, who had very little climbing experience, came to the park around sunrise. He said it appeared the victim did not have the proper knot on the rope as he was trying to rappel off the cliff. "He's only been climbing a few times. It's a new thing for him. It's only been over the last few weeks," Layton said. (Source: Edited from a report by Tyler Murphy in the *Altamont Enterprise*.)

(*Editor's note: While Thatcher Park is considering opening some areas for climbing by permit, it has not yet adopted any policy and climbing here remains illegal.*)

STRANDED, INADEQUATE EQUIPMENT
Lake George, Rogers Rock, Little Finger

On October 13 my partner (27) and I climbed the route Little Finger on Rogers Rock, a three-pitch 5.5 with a descent by 60-meter rappels from bolted anchors to the right of our route. I brought a 70-meter (9.2mm) single rope, and a 75-meter (5mm) static rope to use as a tagline and pull cord, using a modified Reepschnur technique to rappel and retrieve my rope.

After finishing the climb around 4:45 p.m., we rappelled the first 60-meter pitch, anchored into the second set of rap anchors, and began to retrieve the rope using the 5mm tagline. We were able to pull the tagline about 20 meters but could pull no further. Despite our best efforts, including application of full body-weight force, we could see that the end of the single rope was not moving, roughly five meters above us. We felt it was not safe to ascend the thin line with our 5mm prusiks, and I did not feel safe free climbing up to the end of the lead rope, as I did not have any way to protect against a Factor 2 fall and the rappel was off the route line. Around 5:50 p.m. we saw a passing boat. We decided the safest way down was to yell and ask them to notify park rangers.

The park rangers were able to ascend the mountain via a hiking trail on the backside, set up an anchor, and lower in to retrieve the snagged rope system. The rescue ranger then took us down to the bottom of the remainder of the climb safely. Fortunately, secondary accidents and illnesses were avoided as we both had extra layers, headlamps, water, food, and well-charged cell phones.

Analysis

Although I have employed this method of rappelling, using a thin static tagline to pull a single rope, this experience made it clear that it has several potential drawbacks, particularly with an increased risk for getting the rope stuck during retrieval, due to the bulkiness of the knot. I had assumed the granite slab of Rogers Rock would be clean enough to use this method, but experience proved otherwise. There were several cracks and features on the rock where a knot could have easily gotten caught. Using a double or half rope system would have decreased this risk. Other accidents have been reported with incorrectly tied knots as well. In the future, I will only utilize this method when it is clear that the rappels are clean and there is low friction.

With regard to self-rescue, it may have been feasible to ascend the 5mm pull cord with my 5mm prusiks, but we felt it was too risky. It is possible that I could have safely ascended the rope without incident, but I was less zealous about pursuing this method for the following reasons: (1) risk of the rope becoming unstuck during ascension, and (2) uncertainty about the strength of the 5mm pull cord for ascending, given that it was under significant tension and possibly rubbing against the rock. (Source: Cedric Bien, 28.)

RAPPEL ERROR – ROPES UNEVEN AND NO KNOTS IN ENDS, MISCOMMUNICATION
Adirondacks, Chapel Pond Canyon

On December 18 a climber rappelled off the short end of his rope at 30 feet, fell 20 feet to a ledge, tumbled 20 feet more over steep terrain, and slid another 20 feet on steep snow. He suffered a broken pelvis and torn adductor tendon.

Analysis

A 40-year climbing veteran improperly rigged his rappel in such a way that the ends were grossly uneven and there were no end knots in the rope. The scene was a 90-foot ice cliff, and the climber was using a 60-meter, 7.8mm rope. There was no halfway mark on the rope. The climber had poor communication with climbers on ground. There was no line of sight, so only voice communication. The climber relied on mistaken voice communication that ropes were even and down at the bottom. Lessons:

1. Never climb on a rope that doesn't have the halfway point clearly marked.
2. Never rely on questionable voice-only communication with the ground.

3. Always be mindful of the pie graph showing that 29 percent (highest of all) of rappelling accidents occur because of uneven ropes.

4. Always bring both ends of the rappel rope to the top anchor if ever there is a question of rope unevenness.

5. Always tie separate knots at each end of the rope and feed the rope evenly through the top anchor until the halfway mark is reached.

6. Always use a backup in case the ropes begin to run out of control through the rappel device. (Source: Tom Yandon.)

FALLS ON ROCK (16), INADEQUATE PROTECTION (3), INADEQUATE BELAYS (4), RAPPEL/LOWERING ERRORS (2), FALLING ROCK (1)
Mohonk Preserve, Shawangunks

There were 17 reports from the Gunks in 2013. There were no fatalities, but there were seven serious injuries, along with 10 sprains/strains and other minor injuries. In one case, a spontaneous shoulder dislocation caused the climber to fall.

Fourteen of the incidents happened to lead climbers; there was one rappel error (no knot in rope ends) and one lowering error (protection that rope was threaded through came out) resulting in falls. The rockfall injury occurred when a climber dislodged a rock that struck a climber at the bottom of the cliffs. He was not wearing a helmet, but luckily was only hit slightly in his shoulder. The person who reported this said that he and his partner were the only ones wearing helmets at the base of the climbing area.

The average age of the climbers involved was 38, and the average degree of difficulty of the routes was 5.5. Over half the victims were 35 and above and were experienced. (Source: From reports submitted by Mohonk Preserve and Robert Aspinwall, who observed the rockfall incident.)

NORTH CAROLINA

FALL ON ROCK, PROTECTION PULLED OUT
Hanging Rock State Park, Moores Wall

I witnessed an accident on June 8 that teaches a good lesson and luckily had an okay outcome. The climber was a strong and competent, but new to the area. I watched him easily climb Nuclear Crayon (5.10c R) and Quakerstate (5.10d/11a). After onsighting both he started Stab in the Dark (5.10d).

He pulled the boulder problem off the ground (placing one piece of gear along the way) and climbed up under the low roof about 15 to 20 feet off the ground. At this point there is a crack under the roof where gear can be placed prior to traversing left around the arête to gain the crux crack sequence. He placed a nut and a yellow Alien under the roof, both clipped to the same sling.

After attempting to get established around the arête and place some gear, he decided to retreat to the nut/cam placement and asked his belayer to "take."

As soon as he weighted the gear, both pieces pulled and he fell to the ground, landing flat on his back. It looked like a very hard fall. The three of us in the Amphitheater ran to help. Long story short, he had a small cut on his back, got the wind knocked out of him, maybe a sprained ankle, and an injured tailbone. He decided he was okay and was able to walk out on his own.

Analysis

The horizontal crack under the roof starts out very uniform on the right. Near the left side, where one pulls around the arête, the crack has a narrow opening and slightly widens deeper inside the crack. I believe this is where he had the gear, and had placed a cam that was too small for the crack. It was likely the right size for the opening, but too small once beyond the constriction. The cam inverted (breaking the trigger wires), and the second piece (the nut) was not sufficient to take the weight. The last piece was too low to do anything.

This is a good lesson to make sure there are two solid pieces between you and the ground or a ledge. Climbing with new people, new gear (the gear was not his), and in a new location might have contributed to this incident. (Source: C. Sproul, from a post on Mountainproject.com.)

FALL ON ROCK, FREE SOLO CLIMBING
Pisgah National Forest, Black Fork

A male climber (18) was seriously injured in a fall on August 3 at the Black Rock climbing area, located in the Grandfather Ranger District of Pisgah National Forest, near the Linville Gorge Wilderness Area. He was free soloing Crazy River (5.9) when he fell approximately 60 feet to the ground, fracturing his face and sustaining other injuries.

OREGON

FALL ON SNOW, CLIMBING ALONE
Mt. Hood, West Side

On June 22, Kinley Adams (59), an experienced climber, registered to climb Leuthold's Couloir. It appears that he got off route, crossed the Yocum Ridge, and continued to the upper headwall section of the Sandy Glacier. Apparently he slipped or was hit by falling rocks and suffered a long fall. He was located at 8,400 feet by an aircrew seven days later, after the weather cleared. The next day a ground team battled avalanche and rockfall hazards to recover his body. He was found without helmet or crampons, and significant head trauma was observed. But his use of such protective gear is inconclusive because a climber can easily lose both crampons and helmet during a long fall.

Analysis

Getting off route can make an easy climb very difficult, and inclement weather can often lead to disorientation. Climbers should study route descriptions well to prevent this. Climbing solo adds additional risk to most routes, although this route was well within the climber's ability. Dr. Adams carried a cell phone, but the dynamics of the accident did not allow a distress call. (Source: Jeff Scheetz, Portland Mountain Rescue.)

FALL ON SNOW, CLIMBING ALONE, EXCEEDING ABILITIES
Mt. Hood, Cooper Spur

On August 11, Sebastian Kinasiewicz (32), a Polish military officer reported to be a novice climber, attempted a summit climb via the Cooper Spur route. He was reported overdue. Hood River Crag Rat volunteers were able to find and follow his tracks until they abruptly ended 100 feet below the summit. A Blackhawk aircrew spotted his body on the north face about 1,000 feet below the tracks.

Analysis

The Cooper spur is not considered to be a safe route for a solo novice climber. Further, the route is dangerous in August due to loose rock and extreme exposure. (Source: Jeff Scheetz, Portland Mountain Rescue.)

FALL ON SNOW
Mt. Hood, Hogsback

On November 25, John Andrews (62) fell more than 200 feet into a "crater" (sic) near the Hogsback area, along the south-side route. Andrews' climbing partner used a cell phone to call 911, then remained in contact with the Clackamas County Sheriff's Search and Rescue Unit, which coordinated the rescue.

Portland Mountain Rescue, American Medical Response Reach and Treat Team, and Mountain Wave Search and Rescue set up a command post at Timberline Lodge. Andrews was conscious and breathing when rescuers reached him. After stabilizing Andrews, they loaded him into an Oregon Army National Guard HH-60M helicopter around 6:30 p.m. for a quick flight to Legacy Emanuel. (Source: Edited from a report in *The Oregonian* by Rick Bella.)

(Editor's note: Climbers are often unroped on this route. As a result, the consequences are greater when a fall happens. Also on Mt. Hood, in early August six snowboarders set out on foot to explore an overhanging crevasse at the 8,100-foot level on the White River Glacier when a serac collapsed and buried three of them. Two near the surface survived, but one was buried too deeply and perished. Skiers and snowboarders are reminded that they need to recognize mountaineering hazards.)

FALL INTO CREVASSE – SNOW BRIDGE COLLAPSED, CLIMBING UNROPED
Mt. Jefferson, Whitewater Glacier

Our team—Craig Hanneman (64), Mark Morford (56), Bob Alexander (56), and Jim Walkley (40)—was traversing the Whitewater Glacier at about 1 p.m. on July

20, after successfully summiting via the Jefferson Park Glacier route. We were traveling unroped, and our helmets and crampons were stowed. Conditions on the glacier were such that we believed existing crevasses were for the most part open and obvious and could be easily avoided.

At around the 8,900-foot level, midway across the glacier, we encountered an area of tic-tac-toe crevasses. Hanneman, who had climbed the same route two weeks prior, and Morford were in the lead, and Walkley and Alexander were a short distance behind. Hanneman recognized that we probably had drifted too far down-glacier and needed to climb a little to get around this crevassed section. Alexander suggested roping up, and we were beginning to back out of the area to accomplish this when the snow under Hanneman gave way. He had been unknowingly standing on a partial bridge. A 10- by 25-foot section collapsed, and he fell approximately 30 feet into a tapering part of the crevasse. The bridge on which he was standing was probably five feet thick and stayed mostly intact. It wedged in the taper about 30 feet from the surface. Hanneman rode this bridge down. A large portion of the lip followed the main slab and fell on top of Hanneman, mostly burying him. Another large portion of the bridge, about 10 by 10 feet, remained hanging and threatened to fall on him.

The team was relieved to hear Hanneman's muffled calls for help. He was able to partially free one arm after about five minutes and clear a space in front of his face to breathe, but was otherwise unable to move. The rescue effort was dealt an immediate blow when we realized that our one 9mm rope was with Hanneman, in his pack, buried. A quick inventory of every runner, piece of cord and webolette on our harnesses allowed us to cobble together about 40 feet of line. Morford volunteered to go in, but before that could happen we needed to get to the far side of the crevasse. The near wall still had significant amounts of snow clinging to it. We couldn't risk knocking it loose and dropping it on Hanneman.

We did an end run of the crevasse field and then carefully navigated back to the opposite edge of the crack that held Hanneman. Morford tied into our makeshift rope and was lowered with a hip belay into the crevasse. The sides of the crevasse were vertical or overhanging and coated with rotten snow. It was not possible to get any purchase with crampons or tools in the crevasse walls. Thirty minutes had passed since the accident. Hanneman was clad in a T-shirt and was soaking wet, buried in snow, and getting very cold. Most of his body was buried below a block of ice. His head was contorted at an angle that suggested a neck injury. He was conscious but incoherent. It took another 30 minutes to dig him free, access his pack, add some layers, and send the climbing rope up.

Alexander and Walkley set up a haul system in a cramped field surrounded by crevasses. At that point we were fortunate to flag down two other climbers. These two provided extra horsepower and much more assistance. The raise went quickly, but the lip presented us with a difficult problem. Even with an ice axe as edge protection, the rope dug deeply into the rotten snow of the freshly formed lip. Hanneman is not a small guy (6-feet-3-inches and 210 pounds), he had basically lost the ability to control his limbs, and was mostly delirious and in considerable pain. He could do little to assist us in getting him over the last few feet. A second drop loop and a lot of yanking on his arms and harness finally got him over the edge. Close to two hours had passed since the initial fall, and we had a severely hypothermic, injured friend.

Some us worked to get Hanneman out of wet clothes while the others extracted Morford. He too was a little cold after having spent an hour and a half in a wet crevasse. Now in dry layers, Hanneman was placed in two sleeping bags and zipped into a bivy sack. He continued to shiver uncontrollably, flail

[This page] Mt. Jefferson and the Whitewater Glacier under winter snow. *Steph Abegg*

around, and didn't always seem to recognize us.

Despite having a clear view of most of central Oregon, we had been unable to get a cell signal to call or text for assistance. At this point, Kasey Crockett and Tony Chenier (the two other climbers) basically emptied their packs of anything we could use, noted the coordinates of our location, and headed for the Whitewater Trailhead to report the accident to authorities and a fifth member of our party who had elected not to climb. They completed this task by 5:20 p.m. Meanwhile, Morford and Walkley made a round trip to our camp on the North Ridge to collect additional gear for a bivy on the glacier.

Over the course of the evening, as he warmed up, Hanneman's mental state improved, but he was still in considerable discomfort and we worried about possible internal injuries. Our plan was to monitor him through the night and reassess our situation in the morning. We didn't anticipate any assistance until daylight. As darkness fell we all retreated into our bags and tried to stay warm. Hanneman was cocooned in three sleeping bags atop a down air mattress, and all of this was packaged in a bivy sack.

At 11 p.m. we were surprised to hear rotors and see the spotlight from an Oregon Army National Guard Blackhawk. We scrambled to put on our boots and secure our gear. Soon the flight medic was descending, followed by a litter. The helicopter withdrew while we packaged Hanneman, then returned to take him on a wild ride into the sky. The medic grabbed Hanneman's pack and clipped onto the cable a few minutes later. Once he was onboard, the Blackhawk turned away and it was suddenly quiet, except for the sound of one large collective exhale.

Analysis

We should have been roped up when we stepped onto the glacier. There was no reason not to be. The rope had been used appropriately up to this point.

However, we were nearing the end of what had been a straightforward climb and thinking that all of the difficulties were behind us. We just let our guard down. A rope may not have prevented the accident, but it likely would have minimized the injuries and would certainly have expedited the extraction.

We are all grateful for the selfless assistance provided by Kasey Crockett and Tony Chenier, and to the Oregon Army National Guard for their swift response and willingness to conduct a night operation. Our thanks also go out to SAR officials from Linn, Marion, Jefferson, and Deschutes counties for making the right things happen. Finally, our appreciation to the mountain rescue organizations and ground teams that began to mobilize on our behalf. (Source: members of the climbing party.)

FALL ON ROCK – RAPPEL ERROR
Smith Rock State Park, Wherever I May Roam

On May 11 at 5:15 p.m., Deschutes County 911 received a call from Ryan Orr (29) reporting that his climbing partner, Kathy Pawelski (34), had sustained injuries after falling on Wherever I May Roam (5.9). Orr said that Pawelski had fallen about 30 feet while rappelling, and that the two of them were stuck on a narrow ledge about 300 feet from the ground and about 200 feet from the top of the rock face. He advised she was not able to continue her descent and requested assistance.

The Deschutes County Sheriff's Office was notified, and three sheriff's deputies and 15 volunteers from the Deschutes County Sheriff's Office Search and Rescue (SAR) responded to Smith Rock State Park to assist the Redmond Fire Department with the rescue.

Shortly after 6 p.m., the first SAR volunteers arrived on scene and began the rescue. Two SAR members climbed to the top of the rock face, above the two climbers, and rappelled down to their location, while 13 additional SAR members and fire department personnel hiked to the base of the rock face with additional equipment. Pawelski was secured to one of the SAR members, who did a vertical rappel about 300 feet to the rock base. She was then lowered via wheeled litter about 200 feet, down an approximately 50-degree slope, to the trail. At 9:15 p.m. she was transported across the Crooked River and then via ambulance to St. Charles Hospital in Redmond for treatment.

According to an interview that she granted to a local newspaper in July 2013, Pawelski suffered fractures to her skull and right elbow, a concussion, and a spinal fluid leak, resulting in a three-week hospital stay.

Analysis

Wherever I May Roam (5.9) is an intimidating, 500-foot, near-vertical face climb, fully bolted but requiring an exposed series of rappels with a 60-meter rope to reach the ground. As the victim was not willing to reveal the mechanism of her fall, only speculation remains. Did she miss a bolt and rappel off the end of a too-short rappel rope (without a stopper knot)? Did she rappel past a set anchor bolt/rappel point and try to climb back up to it, falling and losing her grip on her rappel ropes? Did she have a backup? The reader can learn a great deal from a study of "Know the Ropes: Rappelling" in the 2012 edition of *Accidents*. (Source: Robert Speik, following interviews with rescuers.)

TENNESSEE

FALL ON ROCK, PROTECTION PULLED OUT, COMPROMISED ROPE-CARRYING CARABINER
Sunset Rock, Chickamauga & Chattanooga National Military Park

On the afternoon of June 30 the park received a report of a serious fall and injury to a male climber (30) approximately one mile from Sunset Rock in the Celebrity Flake area on Lookout Mountain. The climber, who was wearing a helmet, fell approximately 50 feet and landed on his head.

He was approximately 10 feet above his last piece of protection (a nut) when he fell as he was placing his next piece of gear. As he fell the nut below him pulled out. His next piece (a cam) held, but the rope detached from the carabiner attached to a 24-inch runner. The last piece of protection held, the rope stopped him, and he turned him upside down, resulting in his head striking the ground. The impact cracked his helmet. There was enough tension in the rope to leave him hovering approximately three feet above the ground.

Following an hour-long carryout up to the rim of Sunset Rock, he was airlifted to Erlanger Hospital in Chattanooga and admitted with critical injuries. (Source: Todd Milsaps, Chickamauga & Chattanooga National Military Park.)

Analysis

Interviewed witnesses stated that the climber was near his difficulty limit, and they suspected a piece of gear was not placed correctly to stop his fall. What caused the rope to detach from the rope-carrying carabiner attached to the sling? There are several possible explanations, including the possibility that he simply failed to clip the carabiner or the gate stuck in the open position.

Another possibility is whiplash: the rapid opening of a rope-carrying carabiner's gate reacting to a sudden force generated in a fall. This instantaneous opening of the gate can result in carabiner failure if the 'biner is loaded at the precise moment the gate is open. In rare instances it may result in the rope popping through the open gate.

Another potential culprit is back-clipping, which involves clipping the lead rope to a carabiner or quickdraw (which in turn is clipped to protection) such that the rope passes through the carabiner from the front, rather than from the back. When back-clipped, there's a greater chance that the rope could unclip itself from the carabiner during a fall. When done correctly, the rope should pass from the back of the runner or quickdraw and up through the front of the rope-carrying carabiner toward the climber above. (Source: Aram Attarian.)

UTAH

FALL ON ROCK – FATIGUE, INADEQUATE PROTECTION, EXCEEDING ABILITIES
Little Cottonwood Canyon, Beckey's Wall

My daughter Alex (27) had demonstrated very good climbing and protection skills the previous summer when she took me up a two-pitch, 5.7 trad route. Now it was May 11, and neither she nor I had climbed much since. Since she is young and strong (and I am neither at over 70), I thought she could lead Beckey's Wall, a 5.7 trad route on the granite in Little Cottonwood Canyon. However, she had not climbed the route before.

Leading the tricky and slippery first pitch, a ramp in a right-facing corner, I realized she was a bit off her game. But I said nothing, not wanting to interfere. As I watched from the belay anchor, she started up the near-vertical, left-facing corner of the second and final pitch. In my day, one would climb up the corner with a good crack for pro, and then, just before it becomes slightly overhanging, the climber would move left out onto the face where there is—or used to be—a good piton. She placed a good medium-size nut in the corner crack, just below the point where it starts becoming slightly overhanging. She climbed down some and moved out on the face, but could not find a piton. It had been removed. Apparently one is supposed to climb the crack directly now.

I remembered it was possible, but difficult, to place a small nut higher on the face, and suggested she do this. She could not find a good placement of any sort. She decided to go for it, and she climbed through the most difficult section. Now a good eight to ten feet above her last piece, the good nut, she began the traverse back into the corner crack, where it leans back above the steep section. She recalled, "If I fall here I'm in trouble." The traverse is tricky and she was now tired and fell.

I can't recall if I hauled in rope or not, but likely I managed to bring in some, as it is automatic. She rotated to face out, and the rope came tight just as she reached the sloping ramp, barely touching it, about 10 feet above me. She immediately pulled her left shoe off and said she had broken her foot, apparently having hit the wall on the way down. Had she hit the ramp it would have been much worse.

I lowered her to me and then down to the ledge at the start of the climb. She slid on her bum, keeping her left leg off the rock. There were a couple of other climbers at the ledge and they volunteered to retrieve the "saving" nut (now framed). Once at the trail, which is initially steep, it was a long "rumping" (arms and bum to move forward) trek to the parking lot, which is actually only a fairly short distance by hiking standards.

She was diagnosed with a shattered talus bone and fractured calcaneus in her left foot. She was non-weight-bearing for 12 weeks and was in a boot for four months. It was a long summer on crutches, and she is not pain-free, but she's still climbing. (Source: Peter Lev.)

Analysis

We thank this experienced climber for reporting. He thinks that one of the factors at work may have been that both parties were trying to please and/or defer to each other. Parents who are climbing with offspring need to consider this dynamic and try to agree when backing off might be the best solution. (Source: Jed Williamson.)

FALL ON ROCK
Little Cottonwood Canyon, Wheels of Fire Direct

On August 2 an experienced climber, David Buckland (46), was out with his son when he took a fall on Wheels on Fire Direct (5.10) in Little Cottonwood Canyon, a route he had done many times before. He pulled a piece on the way down, got flipped by the rope, and slammed his hip into the wall, causing hip and ankle injuries. His son lowered him to the ground and called for help.

Analysis

David wasn't wearing a helmet when he fell and was lucky he hit the wall with his hip versus his head. He had a lot of experience on this route and commented during the rescue, "Things can go from great to a nightmare in seconds." Wear a helmet. (Source: Michael Finger, Salt Lake County Sheriff's Office SAR.)

(Editor's note: Although we typically do not cover canyoneering incidents, we noted one accident in Utah this year that was the result of the victim clipping her rappel device into the wrong part of her harness. She clipped the elasticized "rope keeper" instead of the belay/rappel loop. The rappeller fell 40 feet and suffered serious injuries. This has application to all rappels. See the photo on this page.)

[This page] In a Utah canyoneering accident, a rappel carabiner was incorrectly clipped to the "rope keeper" on the harness, as shown here. Only the belay loop should be clipped for belaying or rappelling. *Erik Rieger*

WASHINGTON

AVALANCHE, FALL ON SNOW/ICE – INADEQUATE EQUIPMENT, INADEQUATE PROTECTION, WEATHER, EXCEEDING ABILITIES
Mt. Rainier, Liberty Ridge

On the morning of May 18, we (Cory Smith, 26, author of this report; Sydney Seyfart, 30; and Tim Smith, 23) were at about 13,000 feet on Liberty Ridge, just above the Black Pyramid. We were 1,100 feet below the summit of Liberty Cap and the end of the technical terrain. The night before we finished the last of our stove fuel. Two nights before we had discovered frost nip on my brother's toes. We had been on the move since May 14, often through harrowing terrain. The weather had for the most part consisted of pervasive cloud cover that made for poor visibility. This made navigating the Carbon Glacier difficult. We had had to spend an extra day at Thumb Rock due to inclement weather.

Tim led a serac pitch, and then we simul-climbed an ice and snow slope above. There was one last steep, traversing pitch of 55- or 60-degree ice before easy terrain and the top of Liberty Cap. I had chosen to bring only two ice screws on this climb, and when I reached the foot of the final steep ice section I had only one left. The second was on my brother's harness below me. I chose not to set a belay and tried climbing the pitch.

As I only had one ice screw I conserved it, climbing high above a snow picket at the base of the ice. Above the steep ice band I reached a section with ice on the left and snow on the right. I moved to the snow to rest. I should have set the screw before venturing onto the snow. Tim and I were on opposite ends of a 60-meter rope, and Sydney was tied in the center. Because of the traversing, we were zigzag on the slope, with me directly above Tim and Sydney off to the side. As I stomped out steps, I triggered a small avalanche that swept me over an ice band. I fell for 40 feet and fractured the talus bone in my left ankle. My fall continued in tomahawk fashion down the slope between Sydney and Tim. Tim hunkered down on his tools and was hit by the avalanche while Sydney was out of the avalanche path. She had little time to react, and when the rope came taut I ripped her from her stance, along with the snow picket beside her. After the snow passed Tim, he looked up and saw Sydney fall past him, so he hunkered back down again. When the rope came taut, he was pulled about 10 feet down before arresting the fall.

All told, I fell at least a couple of hundred feet and Sydney fell at least 100 feet. Sydney suffered a laceration and bruising above her left kidney, perhaps from the snow picket that popped beside her. I knew my ankle or leg had broken as I fell. When I came to a stop I saw that it was angulated 45 degrees medially. There was no pain or blood.

I was on my side, facing downhill with the rope wrapped around me, constricting my breathing. I righted myself and tried to untangle from the rope, but with my broken ankle this was too difficult. Sydney was yelling above me, trying to figure out if I was OK. "No," I answered, "my leg is broken." I planted my picks in the slope above me, with my lanyards taut on my harness, and then I untied, unwound the skein, and tied back in.

I knew that I had to try to climb out, for several reasons. First, Tim and Sydney weren't going to leave me. Second, we had no way of contacting help and there were no other teams on the north side of the mountain. Third, remaining in our current location would require spending a night out on a 50-degree slope. (Our previous bivy was farther away than Liberty Cap, and reaching it would have required rappelling the serac and giving up precious progress.) Fourth, remaining in technical terrain would endanger the lives of any rescuers who tried to help us, whereas the terrain on top of Liberty Cap was relatively innocuous.

The climbing was slow at first, but I developed a system involving the knee of my bad leg. (My kneecap later suffered cold injury because of this.) Sydney and Tim climbed until they reached the base of the ice band, where Tim set a belay. I reached the belay with some groveling and sat down on a snow bench Sydney had made. I gave my ice screw to Tim, and we decided he would lead the ice band. He completed a phenomenal lead and didn't rest in any snow. Sydney set off after Tim, who had set a belay out of sight. When the rope came taut on my harness, I didn't know what I was going to do, but I knew this traversing pitch would be decisive. Tim and Sydney couldn't assist me, and using my left crampon was out of the question. On hard ice, my left knee didn't work for anything but balance. However, it went better than expected, and once I finished the traverse they were able to assist my ascent. I set three points and yelled, "Pull!" They hauled on the rope and I moved.

Once I reached the belay, Tim began breaking trail through deep snow toward the summit of Liberty Cap. I crawled and scooted along to reach it, then descended the other side to a bivy site. It was about 7 p.m. now, and our bivy site was on a large level area on the ridge descending from Liberty Cap toward its saddle with the Columbia Crest.

They set up the tent with trekking poles because the tent poles had been thrown from my backpack in the fall. I lay down and did nothing, like a Samuel Beckett character. I still was not in pain. In the tent Sydney concluded that instead of going down the Emmons Glacier as we had planned, she and Tim needed to go to the summit early in the morning and make contact with guided parties that could get us help. At the time, Sunrise Road had not yet opened and Camp Schurman was not yet staffed, so the Emmons Glacier was deserted. From the summit they would go down the Disappointment Cleaver route on the southeast side of the mountain. I would remain in the tent and await rescue.

The next day the weather was serene, the best yet, and Sydney's plan worked. Tim and Sydney left me with all their food and water, thinking that I might be there for several days. They subsisted on the generosity of guides, rangers, and other climbers on the DC that day. Three hours after Tim and Sydney left the tent, three guides from IMG and RMI arrived and gave me medical attention, chocolate, tea, and food. They coordinated a rescue with the Rainier National Park rangers and U.S. Army Reserve 214th General Support Aviation Brigade. The area beside my tent served as a landing zone for a Chinook. I was flown off Liberty Cap at 3 p.m. I am indebted to all the individuals, guiding companies, and government organizations involved in my rescue. I am still more grateful to Tim and Sydney for saving all our lives.

Unfortunately, Tim's frost nip turned to frostbite. When he was assessed at Camp Muir, the rangers decided that he should not walk anymore, so they tobogganed him down the Muir Snowfield to Paradise and a waiting ambulance. Four months later, he had to have amputations of the first, second, and third toes of both feet. Sydney was the only one of us to descend the mountain under her own power.

Analysis

There are a number of ways we could have approached this climb to be better prepared and to decrease risk, including asking ourselves several questions more seriously beforehand:

1. Was it reasonable to expect to navigate the Carbon Glacier and ascend Liberty Ridge in potentially poor conditions when none of us had climbed the route before?

2. If so, should we have brought more provisions, fuel, and equipment than we would have brought if conditions were ideal?

3. Should we have considered alternative, less committing routes in the area?

4. Given the route's isolation, would a sat phone or SPOT device have been useful?

If we had brought more fuel, we would not have run low on water. Our initial itinerary was for a four-day climb, and we brought food and fuel for five days. But we ended up spending six days on the mountain. If we had brought more ice screws, I might not have run it out on that final ice pitch, risking a catastrophic fall. Ascending the ice slope above the Black Pyramid would have been faster and safer with more screws. I could have evaluated the slope more conservatively and avoided the snow patch.

So how did Tim lose six toes to frostbite? Two additional, unanticipated days on the mountain increased the duration of his exposure to cold. Due to inexperience, Tim had brought cotton socks for his extra pair. Tim lent his first pair to Sydney on the third day and was unaware that his extra cotton pair would get wet and freeze. When we crawled into our tent during the last two nights, his socks had frozen to the toe boxes of his boots. During the climb, we were unaware of his cotton socks. Sydney and I should have been more involved in Tim's pre-climb preparation. We knew that Tim was the least experienced mountaineer, but we failed to properly compensate for his inexperience during our preparations. Tim met up with us shortly before the climb and we went straight to Rainier. We should have taken the time to inspect his gear.

For Sydney, Tim, and me, this climb was pivotal on a lifelong scale. This was an accident that should never have happened. (Source: Cory Smith.)

INADEQUATE EQUIPMENT – NO SUNGLASSES, SNOW BLINDNESS
Mt. Rainier, Camp Muir

On June 8, a little before 7 a.m., rangers at Camp Muir received notification of a 32-year-old female climber from New York City having difficulty opening her eyes due to pain and swelling. Rangers assessed the individual and determined her eye problems were most likely due to snow blindness; she hadn't worn sunglasses during her hike to Muir the previous day. The patient was unable to open her eyes and complained of significant eye pain (7 out of 10) but had no other injuries. As she could not see and was unable to safely descend, even with assistance, rangers initiated a carryout. (Source: Mt. Rainier ranger report.)

WEATHER – BENIGHTED, EXCEEDING ABILITIES
Mt. Rainier, Liberty Ridge

On June 23, climber Patrick Moore (52) dialed 911 from his satellite phone around 5 p.m. Patrick and his partner, Peter Roach (mid-40s), had climbed Liberty Ridge in deteriorating weather. The ascent took them longer than planned, and incoming weather reduced visibility. Patrick and Peter felt uncomfortable navigating the descent of the Emmons/Winthrop Glaciers route. Dispatch transferred the call to Ranger Payne at Camp Muir, who advised the party to ascend to the crater rim and set up camp for the night, then descend the Disappointment Cleaver route when conditions improved in the morning. He advised against navigating at night in poor visibility. The climbers descended in the morning, passing Camp Muir by afternoon. Ranger Hutchins provided transportation from Paradise back to their vehicle at White River Campground.

Analysis

The party of two did not have sufficient skills to navigate their intended route in the weather that occurred and did not have an appropriate backup plan if weather changed for the worse. (Source: T. Payne, Ranger.)

FALL ON SNOW – SKI MOUNTAINEERING
Mt. Rainier, Emmons/Winthrop

On July 7 a nine-person ski-mountaineering party from Canada summited Rainier via the Emmons/Winthrop Glaciers route. On the descent, one member of the team (47) fell while skiing and sustained multiple traumatic injuries. He landed in what's known as the Alpine Meadow, a flat area near 13,500 feet on the Winthrop Glacier. Some team members stayed with the patient while others descended to Camp Schurman for help. Park dispatch was notified via SPOT beacon, 911 calls, and the emergency radio at Camp Schurman. Ranger Payne was notified by dispatch at 3:07 p.m.

Ranger Payne assumed incident command and put together a response team. A field team of two climbing rangers was picked up from Camp Muir via Chinook helicopter and inserted 30 minutes from the accident scene at Liberty Saddle. Upon accessing the patient, Ranger Self determined the patient needed immediate extraction. The patient was flown to Madigan Hospital.

Analysis

However well prepared a party is for navigating the upper mountain, success depends on skill, experience, and judgment. Ski mountaineering allows less room for mistakes than conventional climbing. Climbing Mt. Rainier can be made safer in places by using skis, but if used unwisely skis can make climbing more risky. The trick is to know when one needs to remove skis and rope up, when to rope up with skis, and when to remove skis, rope up, and use standard glacier climbing techniques.

Using skis to ascend glaciers during the winter—and even into May and June, when the snow is deep, warm, and soft—can help decrease the chances of a crevasse fall. The skier's weight is spread over a larger area, and skis decrease the time spent on a snow bridge. During descent, skiers traveling at 10–15 mph are often not over a crevasse long enough to fall in.

Traveling in a rope team on skis requires additional skill. Parties should practice this technique and test their ability to stop a fall in safe areas with variable snow conditions and slope steepness. Self-arresting on skis is not the same skill as stopping falls while climbing on foot.

There is a misconception among those who are not ski mountaineers that skiing is significantly more dangerous than climbing. While skiing can be dangerous, when techniques are used wisely it can also be a safer way to climb Mt. Rainier. This party simply chose the wrong technique for the particular conditions. (Source: L. Veress, Ranger.)

FALL ON SNOW (CREVASSE JUMP), EXCEEDING ABILITIES
Mt. Rainier, Emmons/Winthrop

On July 21 at 1:30 p.m., mountain guide Chris Watson reported an injured climber via 911. Watson, who was with another guide, reported that Rody Senner (31) had jumped over a crevasse at 11,300 feet on the Emmons/Winthrop route. She sustained a possible tibia-fibula fracture. Watson reported Senner was stable but not ambulatory. She was climbing with two others, including party leader Alex Mondan, who had previously climbed the mountain via multiple routes.

Analysis

Senner was descending the Emmons-Winthrop route when the leader of her climbing party jumped across a crevasse. She followed suit but upon landing felt her right ankle roll and heard an audible crunch. She was wearing crampons. She felt that the jump was too much, given her abilities. (Source: Ranger Worstell.)

SEIZURES – COMPLICATIONS FROM HACE, PRE-EXISTING CONDITION
Mt. Rainier, Disappointment Cleaver

On August 17 at 5:30 a.m., an RMI guide (Dave Hahn) called Enumclaw dispatch and reported that he was guiding a 19-year-old client who had gone into seizures at the top of Disappointment Cleaver. The patient was short-hauled and then transferred to an air ambulance for definitive care at Harborview Hospital.

Analysis

The patient "had a history of brain tumors." (Source: Mt. Rainier ranger report.)

(Editor's note: While not a climbing accident, this report is included to point out the importance of disclosing previous medical conditions to guides and/or fellow climbers.)

WEATHER – OVERDUE
Mt. Rainier, Emmons/Winthrop

On August 25 a private party of five climbers led by Marcos Franco (23) attempted to summit Mt. Rainier via the Emmons/Winthrop route. While descending from the summit, they experienced high winds and low visibility and decided to shelter in place. The following day they were unable to descend, due to inclement weather. On August 27 climbing rangers reached the party at 13,100 feet and led them to Camp Schurman, where they rested overnight. A team of volunteers from the Seattle and Everett mountain rescue associations climbed to Camp Schurman to assist. All parties were out to Glacier Basin by 11:30 a.m. on August 28. After medical assessments of two individuals, it was determined that no serious injuries had been sustained by the overdue party, and they self-transported from the scene.

Analysis

This party did many things right. They practiced together. They hiked to Schurman together during their training. They climbed Mt. Adams together. A member of their party had been to the summit before. This party's main failure was not planning for the weather (which was unseasonably unstable during the period). They had a GPS but did not get GPS tracks on the way up or place any waypoints. They also did not carry any wands.

Once they summited around 11 a.m., the weather deteriorated and obscured their descent route. They were unable to descend past 13,900 feet. They spent the night in an igloo they built. The next day they descended another 800 feet, but were unable to find their way down through the maze of crevasses they had come through. They built another snow cave large enough for five people, using their ice axes and snow flukes. When we arrived on scene, I asked them what they were going to do if we didn't come. They said that they would have built a bigger snow cave. (Source: Stefan Lofgren, NPS Ranger.)

FALL ON SNOW, FALL INTO CREVASSE – FATIGUE, UNABLE TO SELF ARREST
Mt. Rainier, Emmons Glacier

A group of three climbers was ascending Mt. Rainier along with our group on August 31. At midnight we left Camp Schurman to ascend the Emmons Glacier. A third of the way up, our rope teams split. We assumed the second party had turned around, as they showed signs of fatigue. We tried to contact them, but the handheld GPRS units we brought were unable to connect. Two-thirds of the way up, we were surprised to notice our friend's party still following us, only 20 to 30 minutes behind. We continued to the summit, lingered for a short time, and began descending. Shortly after leaving we passed our friends and said hello to them. It was a little late in the day, but they seemed in good spirits and we figured everything was fine.

During our descent we tried to set an obvious path so they wouldn't have difficulty routefinding. At one point during the descent we had an exposed 10-meter traverse above a large crevasse. The snow quality was not good there, with thin crust plus 6 cm of powder on top of ice. I remember thinking that it would be a really bad place to slip, but it wasn't very steep, so I didn't think too much of it. The precarious snow bridges elsewhere on the mountain had seemed much more terrifying.

It wasn't until we got near camp, at about 5 p.m., that we spotted our friends again. They were much farther up the mountain than they should have been—about two-thirds of the way. We started eating dinner and boiling water while keeping an eye on them. They made slow but steady progress down. We would lose sight of them every now and then as they moved behind a serac or a similar feature. Around 7:30 p.m. we lost sight of them again, just above the traverse. After about an hour without further visual contact, we started to get worried. The ranger who was supposed to be at the camp wasn't there, and no one was listening on the emergency radio. We called 911 and they connected us to park staff, who said there was a ranger on the other side of the mountain who would come over as soon as possible.

As we learned later, Climber 2 had slipped and was unable to self-arrest, which caught the other two climbers by surprise. They were unable to stop the slide, and all three fell into the large crevasse. They bounced off one side, falling onto a small ledge. Climber 1 broke a collarbone, dislocated a shoulder (losing sensation in the affected extremity), and was confused. Climber 3 had split his helmet in two and was having a hard time understanding where he was. (Subsequently, Climber 3 had no recollection of the weekend.) Climber 2 was more or less uninjured, and he was able to keep the other two safe.

Around 10 p.m. we had all suited up again and packed some emergency gear, and we left camp. A couple of other guys who had climbed Rainier that day stayed back to keep an eye on us. (They were more tired than we were, and we didn't want to endanger too many people.) We got to about 100 meters short of where the other team had disappeared when one of our teammates completely ran out of energy and was unable to move. The situation was very frustrating, but we had to turn around. We ended up having to short-rope him back to camp. On our way down, about 1 a.m., we ran into another party climbing the mountain. We told them about the accident and where the stricken group was. They continued up, finding the climbers around 4 a.m. They were unable to reach the group because they were on the other side of the crevasse, but they sent out a 911 call.

Around the same time a ranger arrived at our camp. At 6 a.m. another party started going up to the accident site while the ranger built a helipad. The rescue party got to the crevasse around 9 a.m., and one of them was lowered into the crevasse to bring the victims some extra jackets and water. They were eventually long-lined from the mountain by helicopter later that afternoon.

Analysis

Arresting a fall on snow, especially in icy conditions, is not a sure thing. Most self-arrest practice is done in fairly ideal snow conditions, and does not take into account factors such as exhaustion and surprise. Tunnel vision was also in play here, as none of the climbers had noticed the crevasse before they fell in. The team was probably excessively tired as well, though this is a difficult thing to assess, as it was not particularly noticeable when we saw them near the summit.

Climbers 1 and 3 were both fairly experienced, and Climber 2 had received all the appropriate training, but had little experience. Overall, the team was well prepared. They had plenty of warm clothing and a bivy sack. It took 15 hours before they received any real assistance, so the extra clothing they had was crucial to their survival.

An additional note: Try to make sure the right people are contacted when one calls 911. It wasn't until the second call, about eight hours later, that search and rescue was actually notified. The first 911 call had reached the park office, but it was closed. (Source: Alan Trick, friend of Climber 1.)

(Editor's note: We received two separate reports on the same incident, and below we offer the second report, from the Rainier ranger staff, for its additional perspective.)

FALL INTO CREVASSE, FATIGUE
Mt. Rainier, Emmons Glacier

On September 1 at 4 a.m., the park received an emergency cell phone call from a team of climbers on the north side of the mountain. They reported that another climbing team, consisting of Canadian climbers Andrei M. Pipas (leader, 31), John Spence, 50, and Oudina Takpharias Chersi, 31, had sustained multiple injuries from a fall into a crevasse at 11,400 feet on the Emmons Glacier. Rescue operations were initiated immediately. The park's short-haul co-operator, Northwest Helicopters, inserted four climbing rangers at a landing zone approximately 100 feet from the scene. The patients were short-hauled from the crevasse and flown to the Sunrise area. Two of the climbers were transported by Airlift Northwest to Harborview Medical Center; the third was transported to a local hospital via ambulance.

According to statements given by Spence, they began their climb from Camp Schurman at 4 a.m. on August 31. They were climbing with two other rope teams from Canada. All three teams summited at 2 p.m. During the descent Spence's team became separated and spent approximately one hour trying to regain the "main" route. Spence said they were all very tired from the climb and the extra routefinding. Around 11,400 feet, Spence, in the middle position on the rope team, slipped or tripped and began to fall. He slid about 15 feet before falling into a crevasse. He stated that he was momentarily able to arrest his fall on the lip of the crevasse, but then was pulled off when Pipas and Chersi fell. They landed in a group on a ledge, about 40 feet down in the crevasse. Spence believes this happened around 5 p.m.

At 3:50 a.m. an independent climbing party of four came on scene and made the 911 call via cell phone. Another party of two arrived on scene and lowered a doctor into the crevasse to give care and provide patient updates.

Because of the nature of the injuries and the location of the incident, the plan was to short-haul the victims from the scene to Sunrise, where they could be transferred to ground or air ambulances and taken to hospitals. A ground evacuation option also was planned, utilizing resources from Olympic and Tacoma mountain rescue.

On September 2, Harborview nurses reported that Chersi was being treated for a liver laceration, fractured transverse processes of the spine, and possible spinal cord/nerve damage to his left brachial plexus, affecting his left arm. He was also initially treated for hypothermia and minor bumps and bruises. Pipas had been evaluated for head trauma, but was due to be released later that day. He remembered summiting, but was unable to remember anything leading up to the accident. (Source: Stefan Lofgren, NPS Ranger.)

(Editor's note: As noted above, this is the same incident described in the previous report, this time from the rangers' perspective.)

INADEQUATE PROTECTION – RAPPEL ANCHOR
North Cascades National Park, Mt. Goode, Southwest Couloir

On July 6 two experienced climbers summited Mt. Goode (9,200 feet) via the northeast buttress. They started their descent via the southwest couloir, a standard descent route. At 8,400 feet, one climber fell when the rappel anchor failed. He suffered an open elbow and arm fracture, among other injuries, and was initially unconscious.

His partner activated a satellite beacon at 9:30 p.m., and then they bivouacked in the couloir for the night. Early on July 7 both climbers were rescued by NPS rangers utilizing a contract helicopter. (Source: NPS Morning Report.)

STRANDED, EXCEEDING ABILITIES
North Cascades National Park, Black Peak

On July 28 a party of four from the Seattle area attempted the northeast ridge of Black Peak (8,970 feet). The climbers split into two rope teams, but quickly found that the first rope team was ascending at a faster pace. The first rope party summited the peak and then descended the south face back to their camp, having lost contact with the other two climbers.

The two climbers who had summited could see their friends about midway up the ascent route, and observed that they were stationary for hours, well into the night. The two stranded climbers began flashing headlamps, presumably to alert their friends. The climbers at camp asked other visitors who were leaving the area to call 911 and request assistance when they got into cell phone range. Rangers received this call for assistance at 2 a.m. on Monday morning. It was unclear if either of the stranded climbers was injured.

Early on Monday, rangers made a recon flight to Black Peak. They made visual contact with the climbers, and were unable to rule out injuries. By then, the climbers had been at the same location for almost 24 hours, just before a steep pitch on the most technical part of the route.

A ranger team, using the park's contracted HiLine Helicopter, evacuated each climber individually to their base camp by short-haul. The rescued climbers appeared shaken up by the experience, but were uninjured. All parties agreed that steep, technical mountaineering routes above massive glaciers are much more difficult than climbs of a comparable grade in a gym, to which they were accustomed. (Source: Edited from an NPS Morning Report.)

FALLING ROCK – FALL ON ROCK, NOT ANCHORED
North Cascades National Park, Forbidden Peak

The body of Tyler Barton (31) from Seattle was recovered in North Cascades National Park on Sunday, September 15, by park rangers, supported by a contracted helicopter from HiLine Helicopters of Darrington. Barton and his partner had summited Forbidden Peak via the west ridge on September 14 and were descending when the accident occurred. Several climbing parties were on the west ridge at the time. As the climber descended a commonly used gully, using a series of rappels, he was hit by a falling rock. This triggered his fatal fall of approximately 300 feet to a rock and glacier moat. He was not anchored when hit by the rock. His partner was uninjured. Climbers who had witnessed the fall hiked out from Boston Basin and notified rangers at 10:30 p.m. Another climbing party aided Barton's partner in completing the descent. The next day, park rangers completed the body recovery via helicopter by midday, delayed the night before due to fog and weather. (Sources: NPS Morning Report and the *Seattle Times*.)

WEST VIRGINIA

FALL ON ROCK, OFF ROUTE, PROTECTION PULLED OUT
Seneca Rock

On April 8, Stephen Robinson (22) was climbing off-route near Orangeaid (5.10b), close to the last pitch of Castor, when he fell after placing a fifth piece of gear. The fall caused his top three placements (a nut, a 0.75 cam, and an offset nut) to pull. This resulted in at least a 40-foot fall, putting him 15 feet below the belay. Robinson struck his helmeted head during the fall, knocking him unconscious for roughly a minute. Regaining consciousness, he climbed up to the belay and realized that he had broken his wrist (articular radial fracture). The pair rappelled and hiked out.

Analysis

Placing a nut instead of the cam and a quickdraw instead of an alpine draw might have prevented the accident. (Source: Stephen Robinson)

FALL ON ROCK, LOWERING ERROR – NEW SITUATION
New River Gorge National River, Fern Buttress, Star Trek Wall

On August 26 my partner Sean (27) and I (28) were climbing Transporter Crack (5.6). Sean set up a Black Diamond ATC-Guide device in guide mode to belay me from above. When I was ready to lower, instead of taking me off belay and switching to a more practical lowering system, Sean decided to practice lowering using the autoblock device. Sean threaded a thin sling through the small "release hole" of the device and redirected it through a carabiner clipped to one of the anchor bolts.

As he began to lower me the tension released slowly, then when the device finally opened all the way it inverted, creating a pulley and causing me to gain momentum. Realizing that I was falling, Sean attempted to brake but couldn't hold my weight due to the increasing momentum. I experienced a virtual free fall for about 30 feet until I landed at the base of the climb.

Luckily, because of the relatively short distance of the fall and the fact that I landed on my butt, I was able to hike out under my own power after my group cleared my spine and checked my vitals. They contacted 911 and the Park Service. A ranger arrived on the scene to help coordinate local EMS and hiked out with the group. I was checked out and cleared by the EMS personnel, and driven out by fellow group members.

[This page] Using the belayer's weight to release a loaded autoblock belay device and lower the second climber. For more control, the brake strand is redirected upward through the anchor. A friction hitch clipped to the harness provides a backup. *Sterling Snyder*

Analysis

There were several oversights that caused the accident. First, Sean had used the lowering technique before, but never in a situation where a climber was being lowered from the top of a route. He had only used the technique for climbers that needed to be lowered a few feet while on belay. To the best of his knowledge, he believed the system would be adequate as a lowering technique in this situation. Not so. I should have clipped into the anchor as soon as I completed the route, and a more practical lowering system should have been implemented.

The primary cause of the fall was that Sean neglected to redirect the brake strand into a carabiner connected to the anchor above. In addition, Sean did not back up the brake strand with a friction knot made with webbing or cordelette, which should have been clipped back to his belay loop. (Source: Daniel Kessler.)

(Editor's note: Black Diamond recommends that belayers use a back-up belay when lowering a second climber with the ATC-Guide in autoblock mode. For example, the belayer can use a Munter hitch on a locking carabiner clipped to the belay loop on his or her harness. Black Diamond has produced a helpful video demonstrating lowering and other techniques using this device; search "ATC Guide" at YouTube.)

FALL ON ROCK
New River Gorge National River, Endless Wall

On September 14 a female climber (30) made her first trip to New River Gorge. She fell while leading Totally-Clipse (5.8) on Endless Wall. After placing protection she attempted a move, lost her hold, and fell. During the fall she remembered catching her right foot, injuring her ankle. Her gear held, preventing her from hitting the ground. She came to rest against the wall and was lowered to the ground by her belayer. The pair applied a makeshift splint and attempted to self-rescue. Eventually, realizing this was not possible, they called 911.

Rangers responded, repackaged her for a litter raise, and, with assistance from the Fayette County Rope Rescue Team, raised her about 90 feet to the cliff top. Rangers and volunteers carried her about a mile to a waiting ambulance. (Source: edited from an NPS Morning Report.)

Analysis

Falling is an inherent risk in climbing. The pair should be commended for attempting a self-rescue. (Source: Aram Attarian.)

[This page] Separate stopper knots should be tied in each rappel rope to prevent twisting. *Erik Rieger*

RAPPEL ERROR, NO KNOTS ON ENDS OF ROPE
New River Gorge National River, Star Trek Wall

On Monday, September 23, National Park Service rangers responded to a climbing accident at Star Trek Wall. A male climber (age unknown) had rappelled off the end of his rope and fell about 35 feet. He sustained lower limb and back injuries in the fall. Rescuers had to carry the victim out of the area more than one mile over rough terrain. The victim was loaded onto a helicopter and flown to Charleston Area Medical Center. (Source: NPS Morning Report.)

Analysis

A pre-rappel check should always include you and your partner(s) double-checking the anchor and visually inspecting the ropes to be sure they reach their intended destination, and that the rope ends are even and each have stopper knots. Check the rappel device to make sure that it is set up and oriented correctly; check the carabiner gate (locked); and assess the need for a back-up. (Source: Aram Attarian.)

WYOMING

STRANDED – KNEE JAMMED IN CRACK
Vedauwoo, Easy Jam

On April 21 a climber (mid-20s) got his knee stuck in the crack of a 40-foot climb called Easy Jam (5.4) on the Nautilus formation. Neil Mathison, on duty as Albany County Sheriff's deputy, and Rick Colling, of the Wyoming Highway Patrol, were on scene by 4 p.m. Mathison, who is experienced in high-angle rescue, reached the subject and ensured that he was anchored to the rock. Mathison then attempted to loosen the climber's knee without success. He called for help from local climbers with the Medicine Bow Nordic Ski Patrol.

Ski patrollers arrived on scene with additional climbing and medical equipment by around 7:30 p.m. They ascended via an adjacent route (Cornelius, 5.5), set up a Z-rigged raising system at the top of the climb, and gave the subject some motor oil to lubricate his leg. They extricated him on the first pull. His leg was scraped, bruised, and sore.

Analysis

Some knowledge of climbing self-rescue within the party might have eliminated the need for an organized rescue. Because the climb is short, one rope would have been sufficient to establish a raising system above the stuck climber. (Source: Myron Allen, member of Medicine Bow Nordic Ski Patrol.)

FALL ON SNOW – POOR SNOW CONDITIONS, GUIDE DISTRACTION
Grand Teton National Park, Grand Teton

On June 17, after climbing the Grand Teton and descending in the shade on hard, frozen snow with crampons, we came across an area that had been in the sun for less than an hour. We were 10 meters above a large ledge. We moved over to follow the footsteps we had used during the ascent. As we descended my right footstep collapsed. I attempted to regain my balance but found myself on my right side and sliding for the ledge just above the "Rosenberg Slot." I slid about two or three meters, anticipating sliding in control to the ledge and stopping. As I hit the ledge, my left crampon caught and stopped, but my right foot did not stop at the same time. This resulted in a severe sprain of my left ankle (complete rupture of both peroneus tendons, requiring surgical repair). My climbing client, Mathew, was able to assist me with removing my crampons (we would be out of the snow for the rest of the descent).

I continued to guide Mathew down to the base of the Black Rock Chimney, at which point I called the Exum office and told them I had injured my ankle and would need help getting Mathew down from the Lower Saddle. Jim Springer from the Grand Teton climbing rangers called me on my mobile, and we discussed the options of staying put or continuing to descend until a helicopter was available to assist. Mathew and I continued with a second party that was descending as well. Together we were able to rappel to the bottom of the "Briggs Lab" and then to the area below the "Water Hole." Mathew and I continued down to the Black Dike. Mathew headed to the Lower Saddle to retrieve my ski poles. Just after he arrived, the NPS helicopter arrived with two rangers. They brought a pair of forearm crutches that helped immensely. As we descended, arrangements were made to fly an Exum guide to the Lower Saddle to walk Mathew back to the trailhead and fly me to the valley. Upon landing at Lupine Meadows, I was met by rangers and my partner, who drove me to St. John's Medical Center.

Analysis

Be vigilant when entering into areas of transition between shadow- and sun-affected snow. Be extremely careful when wearing crampons and sliding, even when you feel you are in control.

The distraction of guiding may have caused me to not see the failing snow step that broke out and caused me to slide. I believe I looked back to make sure Mathew was following at the time I lost my balance. This distraction may have contributed to the accident. Traveling in familiar terrain may have contributed to the willingness to multi-task at this point. (Source: Jim Williams, 58.)

FALL ON ROCK – VERY LARGE HANDHOLD BROKE FREE
Grand Teton National Park, Mt. Owen, Crescent Arête

On June 20 at 2:26 p.m., Teton Interagency Dispatch Center transferred an emergency cell phone call from Jeff Judkins (38) to Rescue Coordinator G. Montopoli. Judkins was climbing on the Crescent Arête (Grade III, 5.7) of Mt. Owen with climbing partner Brian Smith (37). He was several rope pitches up and lead-climbing when a door-sized rock that he was holding onto broke free. Judkins fell about 15 feet before impacting a steep rock slab, and then continued to fall another five feet or so before his climbing protection and climbing partner caught him. Neither climber was struck by the rock when it fell, but Judkins stated that he had sustained injuries to his left knee (patella) and right ankle (5 to 6 on a pain scale of 10); that he was able to rappel vertically (he had completed two rappels already); that he would not be able to negotiate less steep terrain; and that he would not be able to hike out. The party was still on the steep upper section of the climb and had about four more rappels to negotiate.

Montopoli queried Judkins about large ledges below him, and was told one was a short distance below. Montopoli told Judkins that once he and his partner reached that ledge, they should stay there and that rangers would probably remove him (and possibly the partner) from that ledge, at close to 11,000 feet. Judkins was instructed on how to prepare for the extraction.

At about 2:30 p.m., Montopoli initiated a rescue response. Grand Teton National Park rangers and the contract helicopter (26HX) with pilot C. Templeton were already at the Lupine Meadows Rescue Cache, having just completed training exercises. Dr. W. Smith, medical adviser, was informed of the situation and consulted several times during the course of the operation.

At about 3:14 p.m. the helicopter, with Rangers D. Jernigan and J. McConnell inside, departed Lupine Meadows on a recon mission to locate the climbing party. At 3:23 p.m. they located the climbers and returned to the Rescue Cache to configure for insertion and short-haul. After significant discussion at the Rescue Cache, the team decided to insert two rangers to the climbers' location on the ledge and remove them one at a time, accompanied by rangers. (The uninjured climber could not be left there alone and would have had to be accompanied by a ranger in an extremely dangerous descent if the decision to also extract him had not been made.)

Helicopter 26HX departed Lupine Meadows at 4:35 p.m. with McConnell spotting and Rangers N. Armitage and D. Jernigan suspended below the helicopter on a 150-foot rope in insertion mode. The rangers placed Judkins in a screamer suit and then extracted him, suspended below the helicopter on a 150-foot rope. Ranger Armitage accompanied him. They arrived at Lupine Meadows at about 5:07 p.m. Climbing partner Smith was then extracted. (Source: George Montopoli, Incident Commander.)

Analysis

There is no mention of whether Judkins tested the large hold before it came loose. (Source: Jed Williamson.)

LOSS OF CONTROL – VOLUNTARY GLISSADE
Grand Teton National Park, Hanging Canyon

At 3:45 p.m. on July 12, I (Ron Johnson) was notified of a request to assist an injured person in Hanging Canyon. The climber (first name "Frank") stated that his partner, Loren Hall (33), was at their camp with an injured leg. Frank was descending Hanging Canyon to get help.

Hall had injured his leg around 10:15 a.m. while descending from a successful climb of the Jaw. They were sit-glissading on a snowfield just above Lake of the Crags when Hall's lower leg became stuck between the snow and a rock. His leg twisted and he heard a "pop." Hall was flown out, and after additional medical care and consultation with medical control he was transported to St. John's Medical Center by private vehicle.

Analysis

I interviewed Frank at the Jenny Lake Rescue Cache. He stated that Hall and Frank did not have ice axes; however, the slope they were on wasn't very steep and Hall's speed was controlled when he injured his leg. It's not clear if the use of an ice axe would have prevented this accident. They did a good job taking care of the injury and getting back to their campsite. It was a prudent decision to seek additional help. (Source: Ron Johnson, Incident Commander.)

ROCKFALL
Grand Teton National Park, Garnet Canyon

On August 27, at 9:15 a.m., a large rockslide occurred in the South Fork of Garnet Canyon. A single climber was buried and seriously injured when his party of three was caught in the outwash of a gully near the north side of Nez Perce Peak.

The initial 911 call came into the Teton Interagency Dispatch Center at 9:30 a.m. via cell phone. According to the reporting person, Truett Davis, many people were involved in a major rockslide and some were possibly buried. Helicopter 25HX was requested for rescue operations, and based on the initial report a request was made for an air ambulance (EIRMC) to respond to Lupine Meadows. Additional personnel and Jenny Lake rangers were requested to assist. The command post was established at Lupine Meadows SAR Cache.

During this time two SPOT device activations were received. Both were associated with the rockslide incident. One was accurate; the second was off coordinates by approximately two miles.

According to the other two members of the team of three (Kevin Nowack and Dave Williamson), they were attempting to reach the summit of the Middle Teton during a day climb from their campsite in the Meadows. The three started the day by climbing directly above camp. This choice of route deviated from the normal climbers' trail by ascending loose scree onto steep slopes. From a high point, the three men became aware of the need to traverse back to the South Fork of Garnet Canyon. As they traversed a small rockslide occurred near their location. Then, as they were crossing the base of a large chute, a very large rockfall cut loose from a cliff face high above their location.

Nowack and Williamson were able to cross the chute and find shelter under an overhang. Phil White (54) was unable to cross, so he took shelter beneath a large boulder. The majority of the very large boulders in the rockfall just missed his location, but a large number of smaller rocks and dirt filled in around his location and buried him. Once the rocks stopped moving, Nowack and Williamson came to his aid. They were able to dig him out by hand. They pulled about two or three feet of dirt and rock away until he was uncovered. He was badly injured, so they kept him warm and did not move him until others arrived to help.

Exum Mountain guides Mike Shane and Brenton Reagan went to the scene and assisted with medical care until Jenny Lake rangers arrived. It was confirmed that only a single person needed medical evacuation. Around 11 a.m., helicopter 25HX responded to the area with Rangers Schuster, Armitage, and Fletcher. They provided advance medical treatment for White's fractured extremities and possible internal injuries. He was back-boarded, placed in a litter, and prepared for short-haul to Lupine Meadows.

Analysis

Rockfall in the Teton Range is a common occurrence year-round. Over the past several years, multiple large rockslides have occurred in and around Garnet Canyon. Throughout the summer, the northern couloirs of Nez Perce have seen multiple small rockslides. During the previous days, monsoonal moisture had deposited a large amount of rain in the area. The rockslide was most likely due to below-average seasonal snow and the wet conditions. (Source: Rich Baerwald, Incident Commander.)

FALL ON ROCK
Grand Teton National Park, Garnet Canyon, Petzoldt Caves

On September 6, between 5:30 and 5:45 p.m., Edward Tom (40) fell 80–100 feet to his death while scrambling within the camping area known as the Petzoldt Caves Camping Zone. Tom had a two-night camping permit for Petzoldt Caves, but when he arrived a large climbing party already occupied the primary tent pads. One member of that group directed Tom, his climbing partner, and a third climber from a separate group toward the location of additional camping sites. The three continued along a social trail in the direction of a series of walled-in caves underneath very large boulders. The social trail appeared to end at the edge of a large cliff band with considerable exposure. There, the climber from the separate group scrambled up and over a "wet, lichen-covered, slick rock" to regain the main approach trail. Tom's climbing partner thought the move around the rock was somewhat difficult and exposed, with a large chasm below it, so he began looking for an alternate way. At that time it appeared that Tom attempted to scramble down and around the slick rock toward the additional sites. The other two climbers heard the sounds of small rockfall and shuffling, and turned in time to see Tom fall out of sight over the cliff band.

Tom's climbing partner and several bystanders made emergency calls and sent texts for help, and indicated that Tom was unresponsive and not moving. The total vertical fall distance was approximately 120 feet, with a free-fall distance of 80–100 feet. Tom's injuries were severe and not survivable.

Analysis

Edward Tom was an experienced outdoorsman, fully capable of the trip he planned in the Tetons. He had much experience with multi-pitch sport and trad climbing in Boulder, Yosemite, and El Potrero Chico, Mexico. He also had mountaineering experience in South America, including a summit of Aconcagua.

The exact reason for his fall cannot be determined with certainty, as it was not fully witnessed; however, it is likely that he slipped or tripped. During the hike to the Petzoldt Caves Camping Zone, two severe waves of precipitation came through in the form of heavy rain and/or hail—the latter was severe enough to cause Tom and his climbing partner to put on their climbing helmets. The rock that he was climbing on at the time of the accident was very wet. Granite can be quite slippery when wet, even when wearing footwear such as the 5.10 approach shoes with "sticky rubber" that Tom was wearing.

The move Tom was attempting would be described as third-class with very high exposure. This means that even though the climbing is not technically or physically difficult, a fall has serious consequences. Tom was wearing a very large overnight pack when he fell, which would increase the difficulty of successfully completing this particular move.

It is important to highlight secondary causes of this accident as well. The large climbing group that had gathered in the primary tent pad area had permits for the Moraine camping zone, not the Petzoldt Caves. After being caught in the hailstorm, they had arrived at the caves area and were contemplating staying the night due to inclement weather. They had not yet set up any tents when Tom and his climbing partner arrived. One member stated falsely that the group had permits for this zone, and another directed Tom, his climbing partner, and the other climber toward the alternate spots. The fact that this group of climbers was occupying this camping area caused Tom and the two others to search for additional camping spots, ultimately resulting in his fatal fall. (Source: Edited from a report submitted by Sara Beck, Edward Tom's widow, with details and wording from the NPS Search and Rescue Report.)

(*Editor's note: There was another fatality in the Tetons this summer, involving a man who fell on snow and was unable to arrest before falling into a moat. The details are confidential at this time.*)

CANADA

Editor's note: Most reports in this section were drawn from individual park reports and summaries. Robert Chisnall of the Alpine Club of Canada compiled these reports and provided each analysis.

YUKON TERRITORY

STRANDED, WEATHER
Kluane National Park, Mt. Eaton

The events in question occurred between May 7 and May 19. Prior to this, the climbers spent a week in Haines, Alaska, waiting to fly in to the Seward Glacier, during which time storms broke precipitation records for much of southeast Alaska. Forecasts toward the end of this weather cycle projected a significant but short-lived high-pressure system. On May 7 the two-member climbing team was flown from Haines to the lower Seward Glacier (1,129 meters). The party's objective was the east ridge of Mt. Augusta (4,289 meters), reached by a long traverse over Mt. Eaton.

The climbers selected the east ridge of Mt. Eaton instead of the narrow, rocky southwest ridge. One member of the team was older and slower. Mindful of this and the short weather window, the team decided to stash some supplies at an elevation of 2,039 meters in order to make a lighter ascent of Mt. Eaton. On May 10, from their high camp on an exposed foresummit at 2,652 meters, it took the climbers a little more than five hours to cover the three kilometers (nearly two miles) to the main summit of Eaton. During the ascent they encountered false tops, huge mushroom domes, and an undulating, corniced ridge. As the climbing party started its descent from the summit on the same day, cloud cover descended with them. By the time the climbers reached camp, one member of the party had reached his limit and could go no further.

Based on the forecast, the party had expected one more day before a storm occurred. Unfortunately, the climbers found themselves groping in almost total whiteout conditions the next day—an untenable situation in the crevassed and corniced terrain. Hence, they climbed back to their campsite and set up their tent again. With only one day of spare food, the party was trapped for the next eight days due to severe weather conditions. Dealing with the storm became physically demanding due to the combination of cold, dampness, minimal rations, constrained hydration, confinement, and periodic exertion. Their food ration was about half an energy bar each day.

During this time, massive amounts of snow accumulated and the flat summit became a corniced dome. They had to dig out the tent repeatedly and re-pitch on top of the accumulating snow pack. The party had to keep the tent sealed most of the time, so they could not safely use the stove. Consequently, they relied on melting water in their sleeping bags.

A second attempt to descend on May 15 served only to demonstrate their weakened ability to cope with the thigh-deep snow. The climbers contacted Jasper Dispatch by satellite phone, and they were transferred to the Kluane Duty Officer. (Park personnel had been in regular contact with the climbers.) When a brief clearance finally came on May 19, they were extracted by helicopter to Haines Junction in an impressive rescue organized by Kluane National Park. It was several more days before the weather settled fully and their base camp equipment could be retrieved.

Analysis

Team limitations drove the difficult decision not to continue descending late on May 10. They probably put too much reliance on the weather forecast. The weather information came from a collation of various weather sources: Kluane National Park weather models, U.S. National Park Service partners on the Alaska coast, discussions with the park rescue pilot, and direct contact with the climbers at least twice a day in order to assess firsthand observations of visibility and precipitation trends. The eight-day storm was unusual in duration but not unprecedented. It is possible that had the team remained at their low point, instead of re-ascending and pitching the tent, they might have been able to use brief clearances to continue the descent.

ALBERTA

STRANDED – WEATHER
Jasper National Park, Mt. Edith Cavell, East Ridge

In the early morning of August 9, two climbers left the Cavell parking lot at 3:30 a.m. for an attempt on the east ridge of Mt. Edith Cavell (3,363 meters,

Grade III, 5.3). They bypassed rock terrain to climb a snow gully at the start of the route, which added time to their ascent. Once into the more technical rock terrain, they roped up and began to ascend the ridge. Their progress was very slow. By 2 p.m. they reached their highpoint above the big shoulder on the ridge and level with a thin snow band that transects the face at 2,900 meters. It began to rain lightly, and the rock above looked committing, wet, and slippery.

They decided that in their current condition it was too risky to continue up or climb back down. At 2:15 p.m., with a thunderstorm building, they called for assistance on their cell phone. As the weather continued to worsen, with an afternoon buildup around the peak, the subjects were quickly located at approximately 2,900 meters on a good ledge. At 4:30 p.m., two Visitor Safety Technicians were slung to their location and they extracted by heli-sling.

Analysis

The east ridge of Edith Cavell is a long, sustained rock ridge and requires good time management and strong skills in order to complete the route and then descend the west ridge, which has a very long hike out, in a single day. A typical round trip via this route is usually 12 to 14 hours. These climbers made decisions that cost them valuable time and energy, especially in light of a weather forecast that was characteristic for that time of year (thunderstorms building in the afternoon). They were well prepared with all the safety gear to manage the route and undertake a bivouac, but they found it difficult to move efficiently over this terrain, given their skill set, risk tolerance, and degree of fitness.

RAPPEL ERROR/FAILURE
Jasper National Park, Mt. Redoubt, Northwest Ridge

In the afternoon of August 15, Visitor Safety received a call about an overdue solo climber on the northwest ridge of Mt. Redoubt (3,120 meters, Grade III, 5.6) in the remote Tonquin Valley in Jasper National Park. Initial investigation found that the climber had missed his scheduled check-in time using a satellite phone the night before. Visitor Safety Technicians found his vehicle at the trailhead and performed a hasty search of the area, which revealed nothing. The next afternoon, as the weather lifted, the climber's body was located from the air, 500 meters below the summit on a small patch of snow in a gully on the west face. It appeared as though he had been rappelling, but it is not clear what caused him to fall or lose control of the rappel.

The steep walls prevented the helicopter from safely deploying the recovery team right at the site, so three Visitor Safety Technicians were slung to a buttress near the climber, and they climbed broken ledges to access a site above him. From here, a technician was lowered onto the steep snow patch to package and sling the subject off the face.

Analysis

This climber was very experienced and thoughtful. He understood the risk he was taking and had the necessary skills and fitness. He also had a solid check-in plan with his family. By all accounts, the route was well within his skill set, and he had the means to retreat from the route. It appears that this was a rappelling accident, but it is not clear if he had slung a block with his rope and the block failed, if there was a failure of equipment at his anchor, or if the weather played an issue (afternoon thunderstorms and high winds).

FALL ON ROCK – HANDHOLD CAME OFF
Banff National Park, Tunnel Mountain, Gooseberry

On July 21 a party of three was climbing Gooseberry, a seven-pitch, 5.7 rock route. The lead climber was on pitch three when he dislodged a loose handhold. He fell approximately 10 meters and landed on his back, sustaining injuries. One partner climbed up to the fallen climber while the second placed an emergency call to Banff Dispatch. The partner was able to lower the leader to a sloping ledge, where they waited for a rescue.

Two Visitor Safety Specialists were dispatched to the accident scene. By coincidence, the rescue helicopter was in Banff at the time and the two specialists were overhead within about 15 minutes. The first specialist slung into the station below the climbers and rigged an anchor for the second specialist. After the second specialist arrived, the first climbed up to the injured climber. The first specialist then established another anchor and belayed the second specialist up. Over the next 20 minutes, the two specialists packaged the victim with some difficulty into a vacuum mattress and Heli-Rescue Bauman Bag. He was also rigged with a releasable system so that the specialists could safely transfer the climber to the helicopter long-line.

Analysis

The rock on climbing routes in the Canadian Rockies is inherently loose. The climbing team was adequately experienced for the route and was prepared to deal with the emergency situation—for example, safely tying off the fallen climber and knowing the correct emergency telephone numbers.

RAPPEL ERROR/FAILURE
Grassi Lakes, Fiberglass Undies

The climber had prepared to rappel from the top of a sport route. As the rappeller descended she removed the upper three quickdraws. Shortly after that, the climber fell to the ground and landed on her back. It was noted that the rope ends were uneven. One rope end was on the ground, and the other was six to eight meters up. There was no knot in either strand. As the upper end of the rope passed through the rappel device, gravity took over and the rappeller fell.

Other climbers in the area had medical training and immediately began first aid. They also contacted EMS, which was able to attend the scene on foot. Meanwhile, a heli-sling operation was initiated for evacuation of the victim. The climber was slung to EMS, and the patient then carried to the hospital. It was reported that the victim sustained a fracture.

Analysis
It is assumed that the rappeller did not utilize a safety or backup knot (autoblock, prusik, etc.), nor were stopper knots tied into the ends of the rappel lines. As well, no helmet was worn. Had the climber communicated with the people on the ground, the misalignment of the rope would have been brought to her attention.

FALL ON ROCK, ROCKFALL
Keelhaul Wall, Kid Goat
On July 13 a climber dislodged a rock on pitch four of Kid Goat, which struck his belayer on the left ankle, fracturing it. The injured climber phoned for a rescue after a self-assessment. While Kananaskis Public Safety (KPS) was responding, the party of two continued to self-rescue and rappel the route. When KPS arrived on the scene the patient was almost at the base of the cliff. He was then slung from the cliff to a staging area, where he refused additional care.

Analysis
The primary cause of the accident was likely a failure to test holds, probably due to a lack of experience. Rescuers deemed there was an inadequate appreciation of the inherent rockfall hazards for leaders and belayers alike.

BRITISH COLUMBIA

AVALANCHE
Glacier National Park, Sifton Col
Around 2 p.m. on March 24, a party of three began a ski descent of the southwest slope below Sifton Col. It was a mild, clear day with light winds. Two members of the group remained at the top of the slope, while one skied down to assess conditions. The skier triggered a size 2.5 slab avalanche near the middle of the slope and was knocked over and carried down the slope. He was buried under approximately one and a half meters of debris in a natural terrain trap.

The two remaining party members performed a companion rescue and uncovered their unresponsive partner. The patient was moved to a safer location, less affected by possible additional avalanches, and CPR was initiated immediately. One person stayed on scene and continued CPR while the second person skied back to the Rogers Pass Discovery Centre to report the incident.

Parks Canada Visitor Safety Specialists received the report of the incident at 3:25 p.m. The avalanche hazard was assessed, and it was deemed safe to land next to the toe of the avalanche deposit. Two rescue specialists continued CPR with an automated external defibrillator (AED), while a third rescuer remained on lookout for further avalanches. With no signs of life coming from the victim, CPR was discontinued and all personnel were evacuated from the accident scene.

Analysis

The avalanche was likely triggered at a thin spot on a scoured, south-facing alpine slope. After the avalanche, exposed rocks were present on the bed surface. These would not have been visible prior to the event. Shallow, weak spots in the snowpack around rocks are common trigger points for avalanches. The avalanche was triggered on a persistent weak layer consisting of surface-hoar crystals on top of a strong, thick crust. This weak layer, combined with direct solar warming of the surface snow, contributed to the size of the slab that released.

The avalanche released well above the trigger point, and the victim was carried into a depression where the debris piled up. Terrain traps like this depression need to be evaluated carefully, as they increase the consequences of even small avalanches.

The group made a good decision to put only one member on the slope to assess the conditions and have spotters in safe locations. During the ensuing rescue, the two party members showed great foresight by moving the victim to a location less exposed to surrounding avalanche terrain. Rescuer safety is a top priority in every rescue.

Editor's note: The website of the Canadian Avalanche Centre has published a series of very instructive and entertaining online exercises for practicing route selection in avalanche terrain. Find them here: http://www.avalanche.ca/cac/training/online-course/reducing-risk/route-finding-exercises.

[This page] Uto Peak (left) and Mt. Sir Donald in winter conditions. *Steph Abegg*

STRANDED, INADEQUATE EQUIPMENT, INEXPERIENCE
Glacier National Park, Uto Peak

On July 6 about 6 a.m., a party of three left the parking lot to climb the southwest ridge of Uto Peak (2,927 meters). They had some difficulty with the steep snow on the approach to the Uto–Sir Donald col, due to very lightweight footwear, and two group members had limited experience, causing the party to take more time than anticipated on the climb. They reached the summit and began descending the northwest ridge late in the evening. They completed two rappels before being caught by darkness around 9:45 p.m. They soon stopped, planning to rest for several hours.

At about 3:30 a.m. the next morning, it began to rain and snow. Due to the slippery rock and the lack of footwear required for descending steep snow, they decided to rappel down the west face of Uto, rather than continue down the northwest ridge. They had completed several rappels from boulders before realizing they were entering progressively more challenging terrain. They decided to request a rescue.

At 8:14 a.m. on July 7, the group called 911 and the party eventually was transferred to Visitor Safety in Glacier National Park. The climbers reported they were uninjured but hypothermic and dehydrated. The weather at the time was cloudy with fog patches and rain in the valley and sleet above 2,100 meters. The Visitor Safety rescue team located the stranded climbers by air and slung onto a ledge five meters below them. The rescuers climbed up to the party and slung them off the face to the basin below.

Analysis

Better footwear would have sped up the approach on steep snow, allowed more time for climbing, and made the steep snow descent off the northwest ridge a possibility. Crampons may also have been useful as well. Some spare clothing, gloves, and an emergency tarp would have allowed them to spend the night in greater warmth and comfort. On longer alpine routes it is good to set a turnaround time and adhere to it if things take longer than expected.

Recognizing that they were not prepared for the situation they were in and calling for assistance was a very good group decision to prevent further complications. Many phones can call 911 if within range of a cell tower, even if they do not have service through the local provider. When calling 911, identify which national park you are in and ask to be connected directly to Parks Canada Emergency Dispatch to minimize the amount of time it takes for your call to reach the Visitor Safety team. Carrying a SPOT device or other emergency locator beacon is another good option, in case your phone does not work.

FALL INTO CREVASSE, SKIING UNROPED
Yoho National Park, Daly Glacier, Wapta Icefields

A party of three was ski touring over a number of days from Peyto Lake to Sherbrooke Lake on the popular Wapta Traverse. The group left Balfour Hut around 11 a.m. on the morning of March 12, and crossed over the Balfour High Col (approximately 3,000 meters) in the early evening, with near whiteout conditions. After starting to descend the Daly Glacier toward the Scott Duncan Hut, five kilometers away, the team members decided to unrope. At approximately 7:30 p.m. one member of the party fell into a crevasse. Another skier went to the edge, on belay with a rope, and yelled into the crevasse but received no response. The skiers received a weak beacon signal originating 35 meters below, inside the crevasse. A rope was lowered 60 meters, but there was no pull on the end. The two skiers on the surface decided there was nothing they could do, given the darkness and weather, so they left their skis to mark the crevasse, walked up to a flat area above the crevasse, and dug a snow cave at around 2,700 meters. They activated the SOS on their SPOT satellite beacon around 11:30 p.m.

From March 13 until March 15, Parks Canada Visitor Safety (VS) rescue crews tried repeatedly to reach the area, but were unable to access the site due

HOLE INTO CREVASSE

[This page] Rescuers at the scene of the crevasse fall on the Daly Glacier. *Parks Canada*

to unusually stormy weather and high avalanche danger. On March 15, with the weather marginally better, a VS team was inserted near the crevasse by helicopter. They were able to ski up to the accident site, where they discovered a pair of skis near the SPOT GPS location. The team investigated the area near the skis and found an open hole in the crevasse. One VS rescue member looked into the crevasse but could see no clues. An avalanche beacon search did not reveal any signals, and there was no response to shouts. As the helicopter was preparing to bring in more equipment for an extensive crevasse rescue, the pilot spotted a party of two on the surface a few hundred feet above the VS team.

The VS team's priorities immediately shifted to the two survivors, who were soon escorted to the nearby heli-pad. The survivors were evacuated by helicopter in very bad weather and taken to a hospital, where they were treated for minor cold injuries. The weather and avalanche conditions were very poor for the next four days. During a clearing on March 19, crews were able to access the crevasse site and reach the deceased.

Analysis

This incident occurred on a popular ski-touring route that is often undertaken at this time of year. One causal factor was the party deciding to unrope in near whiteout conditions and fading daylight. It is common for parties to ski downhill unroped on glaciers, but skiers should always weigh this decision in light of changing or unfamiliar conditions, snow depths, visibility, and so on. Another factor was the route the party followed toward the Scott Duncan Hut, which was steeper and more crevassed than the route most parties take.

Given their experience level, darkness, and the stormy conditions, the party thought it would be too dangerous to venture down into the crevasse or to continue to Scott Duncan Hut after the accident. These decisions were the right ones, given these circumstances. Under such conditions, it may be possible to descend into a hole to check on a fallen skier or climber, but actually getting someone out of a tight crevasse is a very difficult and technical process. It typically requires more rescue resources than parties have available to them.

The skiers remaining on the surface were prepared to bivouac for numerous days, having sleeping bags, a stove and fuel, food, extra clothing, and navigation equipment. They also had a SPOT satellite device, which was accurate and enabled them to initiate a rescue. Of note, SPOT devices are essentially one-way communication systems. Although Visitor Safety knew there was a call for help, they did not know the nature of the incident. There are many such devices on the market, and their capabilities are steadily evolving. If you purchase one, be sure to understand the limitations of your particular unit.

ONTARIO

RAPPEL ERROR/FAILURE, CLIMBING ALONE
Dryden, Banana Lake

On May 6, a lone climber with 22 years of experience headed out to the Banana Lake climbing area. The pull-off is four kilometers down a logging road, and the walk to the cliff is one kilometer. Between 9 and 10:30 a.m., the climber did some route cleaning and placed two bolts on a new route. He then engaged in some roped soloing. After performing several top-roped ascents, he endeavored to move over to the next set of anchors to climb two more routes before calling it a day. He set up the rope to rappel to the other anchors, about five meters to the left and five meters lower down. He weighted the rope and began to traverse over. About halfway across, he began free-falling for about 15 meters.

The climber did not lose consciousness upon impact. He immediately stood up, noting that he was covered in blood. He removed his harness and began walking down the trail, looking for cell reception to call for help. He was able to make the call as he reached his vehicle, and the ambulance and police were dispatched. The climber sustained a dislocated shoulder, a head laceration, a broken foot, a severely bruised tailbone, minor internal bleeding (which took care of itself within a couple of days), and some minor bumps and bruises.

Analysis

A friend went out to look over the site and retrieve the climber's gear. He concluded that a locking carabiner clipped to the ground-anchor bolt, connected to a figure-eight loop tied in the end of the rope, had become detached. There was no failure of bolts, rope, knots, or the carabiner.

According to the fallen climber's self-analysis: "I've replayed the scene in my head over and over since that day, and though I thought that I had locked the 'biner, I obviously hadn't. From now on I will check the setup on each lap, use an auto-locking carabiner, and make sure everything is backed up. Had I used a backup on the ground anchor, this would not have happened. Plus, I will always wear a helmet."

From the description provided, it is assumed the rappel setup was this: One end of the rope was attached to a ground bolt with a locking carabiner and a figure-eight loop (this attachment was the point of failure). The rope ran up through the top anchors, and the rappeller descended the other side of the line. Rappelling both strands of the rope might have prevented this accident. This would have isolated the lower anchor point from the rappel system.

STATISTICAL TABLES

TABLE I
REPORTED MOUNTAINEERING ACCIDENTS

Year	Number of Accidents Reported		Total Persons Involved		Injured		Fatalities	
	USA	CAN	USA	CAN	USA	CAN	USA	CAN
1951	15	n/a	22	n/a	11	n/a	3	n/a
1952	31	n/a	35	n/a	17	n/a	13	n/a
1953	24	n/a	27	n/a	12	n/a	12	n/a
1954	31	n/a	41	n/a	31	n/a	8	n/a
1955	34	n/a	39	n/a	28	n/a	6	n/a
1956	46	n/a	72	n/a	54	n/a	13	n/a
1957	45	n/a	53	n/a	28	n/a	18	n/a
1958	32	n/a	39	n/a	23	n/a	11	n/a
1959	42	2	56	2	31	0	19	2
1960	47	4	64	12	37	8	19	4
1961	49	9	61	14	45	10	14	4
1962	71	1	90	1	64	0	19	1
1963	68	11	79	12	47	10	19	2
1964	53	11	65	16	44	10	14	3
1965	72	0	90	0	59	0	21	0
1966	67	7	80	9	52	6	16	3
1967	74	10	110	14	63	7	33	5
1968	70	13	87	19	43	12	27	5
1969	94	11	125	17	66	9	29	2
1970	129	11	174	11	88	5	15	5
1971	110	17	138	29	76	11	31	7
1972	141	29	184	42	98	17	49	13
1973	108	6	131	6	85	4	36	2
1974	96	7	177	50	75	1	26	5
1975	78	7	158	22	66	8	19	2
1976	137	16	303	31	210	9	53	6
1977	121	30	277	49	106	21	32	11
1978	118	17	221	19	85	6	42	10
1979	100	36	137	54	83	17	40	19
1980	191	29	295	85	124	26	33	8